NEW GEN. BOOKS
DKB4
12–
+52992
AF817585

Cesar Chavez and the United Farm Workers:
A Selective Bibliography

Cesar Chavez and the United Farm Workers

A Selective Bibliography

by Beverly Fodell

Wayne State University Press, Detroit, 1974

Copyright © 1974 by Wayne State University Press, Detroit, Michigan 48202. All rights are reserved. No part of this book may be reproduced without formal permission.

Published simultaneously in Canada by the Copp Clark Publishing Company
517 Wellington Street, West
Toronto 2B, Canada.

Library of Congress Cataloging in Publication Data

Fodell, Beverly, 1930-
Cesar Chavez and the United Farm Workers.

1. Chavez, Cesar Estrada—Bibliography. 2. United Farm Workers—Bibliography.

Z8164.9.F63 1974 016.33188'13'0973 73-6365
ISBN 0-8143-1502-X

Grateful acknowledgment is made to the Archives of Labor History and Urban Affairs, Wayne State University, for financial assistance in publishing this book.

Contents

Foreword

In 1967 the United Farm Workers Organizing Committee designated the Achives of Labor History and Urban Affairs at Wayne State University. Detroit, Michigan, as the official depository of its historical files. At the same time, Cesar Chavez, the dynamic leader of the United Farm Workers, also agreed to place his personal papers in the Archives. Other individuals and organizations, such as the California Migrant Ministry which supported the work of Chavez and the union, also deposited materials. Consequently, this comprehensive collection of correspondence, office files, photographs, tape recordings, diaries, and other first hand materials will be invaluable to future generations of researchers who seek documentation of the historic contributions of Cesar Chavez and his colleagues.

Because of the sensitive and contemporary nature of the files, the United Farm Workers Collection is restricted for an indefinite period. However, there is much additional source material in the hundreds of articles and books written about Cesar Chavez and the United Farm Workers. In order to meet the needs of researchers, students, and other interested persons, Beverly Fodell, archivist on our staff has prepared a bibliography of published materials. This bibliography represents a substantial revision and expansion of an earlier bibliography on Cesar Chavez and the United Farm Workers which was printed in 1970 and distributed by the Archives of Labor History and Urban Affairs.

Philip P. Mason, *Director*
Archives of Labor History and Urban Affairs

Introduction

This bibliography represents a revision and expansion of the bibliography, *Cesar Chavez and the United Farm Workers*, privately printed by the Archives of Labor History and Urban Affairs of Wayne State University in January 1970. Although the format has been slightly changed, the revised edition includes, except for a few deletions, all the citations contained in the earlier edition, as well as significant articles and books published up to November 1972. A few selected items published after that date have been added.

The scope and purpose of this bibliography remain the same. First, it provides those interested in Cesar Chavez, the United Farm Workers, and the various aspects of the grape and lettuce strikes and attendant boycotts, with a wide selection of readily available published materials, primarily articles, books, and pamphlets. Secondly, references to other materials such as articles in scholarly journals, government documents, reports and position papers, dissertations and theses, are listed for the scholar seeking additional reading or doing more serious and extensive research.

The primary emphasis is on the current organizing efforts of farm workers which began with the grape strike in Delano, California. This strike, started on September 8, 1965 by the Agricultural Workers Organizing Committee, AFL-CIO, was joined eight days later by the National Farm Workers Association, under the leadership of Cesar Chavez. In August 1966, the two organizations merged to form the United Farm Workers Organizing Committee (UFWOC), AFL-CIO. In May 1972, UFWOC was granted independent status by the AFL-CIO and the term "Organizing Committee" was dropped from the union's name.

The bibliography contains separate sections listing bibliographies, government documents, unpublished materials (including theses and dissertations), annual reports and proceedings, books and pamphlets, and periodical and journal articles. Listed are items which refer specifically to Cesar Chavez, the grape strike, the boycotts of wine grape products and table grapes, the lettuce strike and boycott, the United Farm Workers (prior to May 1972, the United Farm Workers Organizing Committee), the Agricultural Workers Organizing Committee (AWOC), and the National Farm Workers Association (NFWA).

Also listed are selected items on peripheral but related general topics such as the importation of foreign farm workers under Public Law 78 (braceros) and Public Law 414 ("green card" immigrants), previous farm labor strikes and attempts to unionize agricultural workers, child labor in agriculture, living and working conditions of migrant workers, agribusiness, farm labor contractors, agricultural mechanization, wages, unemployment and workmens compensation, land grant colleges, the use of pesticides and other chemicals in agriculture, the activities of the Migrant Ministry and other church-related organizations, and federal and state legislation for farm workers.

Bibliographies

The bibliographies selected cover such subjects as agricultural labor, Chicanos and Mexican Americans, collective bargaining in agriculture, farm labor organizing, mechanization in agriculture, and migrant labor. Those bibliographies dealing with Chicanos and Mexican Americans contain numerous entries on farm labor, Cesar Chavez and the United Farm Workers, and related topics.

Among the many bibliographies listed, those of Isao Fujimoto and Jo Clare Schieffer merit special mention. In addition to annotated bibliographic citations, they include several sections dealing with the mechanics of finding various types of materials—information especially invaluable to the serious scholar.

Government Documents

The selected items relate to braceros, UFWOC, Public Laws 78 and 414, the National Labor Relations Act, migrant labor, federal and state labor laws, minimum wage for agricultural workers, farm labor contractors, unionization of farm workers, and living and working conditions of migrant workers.

Especially recommended are Stuart Jamieson's *Labor Unionism in American Agriculture* and the hearings of the Senate Subcommittee on Migratory Labor, *Migrant and Seasonal Farmworker Powerlessness.* Jamieson's dissertation (University of California, Berkeley, 1943) was published by the Department of Labor, Bureau of Labor Statistics, in 1945. It remains one of the most definitive works on the subject of the unionization of farm workers in the United States.

The Senate hearings, frequently referred to as "Farmworker Powerlessness," were designed to "explore the extent to which migrant workers are powerless to influence decisions in both their home base communities and in so-called user States." They include many reports and papers and examine such topics as political and economic power, the migrant culture, border commuter problems, the effects of pesticides, legal problems, community participation, and unionization.

Theses and Dissertations, Annual Reports, Proceedings, and Unpublished Materials

The items selected pertain to Cesar Chavez, the United Farm Workers Organizing Committee (UFWOC), the Delano grape strike, agribusiness, past and present efforts to unionize farm workers, growers' reactions and attitudes, legislation, migratory labor, and related topics.

Books and Pamphlets

Books and pamphlets about, or which mention significantly, Cesar Chavez, the United Farm Workers Organizing Committee, The National Farm Workers Association, the Agricultural Workers Organizing Committee, and the grape strike and boycotts; and selected general references on agricultural labor in the United States, organizing agricultural workers, the importation of foreign farm workers under Public Law 78 and Public Law 414 (McCarran-Walter Immigration and Nationality Act), minimum wage, agribusiness, pesticides, mechanization, the Farm Bureau, child labor, the Migrant Ministry and the role of churches and clergy, federal and state legislation, and related topics, have been included in this section.

Articles

Those articles written prior to the beginning of the grape strike in September 1965, and articles in which the subject matter antedates the beginning of the strike, pertain to selected references about braceros, Public Law 78, Public Law 414, proposed and enacted state and federal legislation, child labor in agriculture, living and working conditions of migrant workers, mechanization, and earlier attempts to unionize farm workers by the Industrial Workers of the World, Southern Tenant Farmers Union, National Farm Labor Union, Agricultural Workers Organizing Committee, and others.

In addition to specific citations contained in the bibliography, the reader should be aware of several other sources:

Newspapers

Among those newspapers which have published many articles and news stories about Cesar Chavez, UFWOC, and the grape and lettuce strikes and boycotts are the *Christian Science Monitor, Delano Record, Fresno Bee, Los Angeles Times, New York Times, Sacramento Bee, Salinas Californian, San Francisco*

Chronicle, Wall Street Journal, and *Washington Post.* There have also been numerous articles in daily newspapers in the United States and Canada where there have been organized grape boycott and lettuce boycott activities. The *California News Index,* which began publication in 1972, indexes the major California newspapers.

Labor Union Publications

The most useful source for articles and news stories appearing in labor union publications through 1968 is the *Michigan Index to Labor Union Periodicals.* Although this index ceased publication with the December 1968 issue, it will still provide the reader with an indication of those labor union periodicals and newspapers which frequently publish articles and news stories about the various aspects of the union movement among farm workers.

In addition, the reader should consult the newspapers of city, county, and state AFL-CIO councils; those of the various international unions; and most especially, *El Malcriado,* published by the United Farm Workers.

Grower Publications

Examples of the various categories of grower publications include the *American Farm Bureau Newsletter, American Fruit Grower, American Vegetable Grower, California Farm Bureau Monthly, California Farmer, Canner/Packer, Farm Journal, Farm Quarterly, Packer,* and *Western Grower and Shipper.* Although many larger city and university libraries have some of these publications, the largest selection of grower magazines, newspapers, and newsletters is at state colleges of agriculture.

Other items which should be consulted are the newsletters or magazines of state Farm Bureaus and the annual reports and proceedings of state horticultural societies, especially in states where large numbers of seasonal farm workers are employed.

Church Publications

Many churches, clergymen, and religious organizations have expressed interest, with varying degrees of support and opposition, in the current organizing activities of farm workers. These interests have often been reflected in the publications of churches and religious organizations, including newspapers, newsletters, and magazines with local, regional, or national circulation. Examples include the *CMM Newsletter* (California Migrant Ministry), *Catholic Post, Engage, National Catholic Register, National Farm Worker Ministry Newsletter, Our Sunday Visitor, Presbyterian Life, Southern California Presbyterian,* and *Twin Circle.* Frequent articles have also appeared in Msgr. George Higgins's weekly column, "The Yardstick," which is syndicated in approximately thirty Catholic newspapers in the United States and Canada.

Abbreviations

The following abbreviations have been used in the annotations to the citations:

AWOC	Agricultural Workers Organizing Committee
NFWA	National Farm Workers Association
NLRA	National Labor Relations Act
NLRB	National Labor Relations Board
UFW	United Farm Workers
UFWOC	United Farm Workers Organizing Committee

Bibliographies

Birdwell, Gladys B. *Chicanos: A Selected Bibliography.* Division for Development of Collections, University of Houston Library, January, 1971. 60 pp.
Contains sections on monographs, journal articles, and government documents. Covers all phases of Mexican American history and culture from the Aztecs and Mayans to Chavez and Tijerina.

California State Library. Law Library. *Strikes and Boycotts: An Annotated Bibliography,* by Armando Venegas. Sacramento, 1970. 8 pp.

Cameron, Colin and Joanne Edelson. *Farm Labor Organizing: An Annotated Bibliography.* Madison, Wisc.: Institute For Research on Poverty, University of Wisconsin, December, 1969. 62 pp.
Includes sections on source materials (indices, bibliographies, government periodicals, newsletters, farm labor presses), housing, helath, education, immigration, legislation, early attempts to organize, contemporary strikes and boycotts, and films and tape recordings.

Cardenas, Gilbert and Ricardo Parra. *La Raza in the Midwest and Great Lakes States, 1924-1973: Selected Bibliography.* Notre Dame, Indiana: Centro de Estudios Chicanos, University of Notre Dame, January, 1973. 8 pp.
Includes references to farm labor and migrant workers.

Chicanos: A Selective Guide to Materials in the UCSB Library. University of California at Santa Barbara, Library, Reference Dept., January, 1972. 78 pp.
Lists bibliographies, books, curriculum development guides, and government publications. The earlier edition (*Mexican-Americans: A Selective Guide to Materials,* 1969) also listed periodical articles.

Clark y Moreno, Joseph A. "Bibliography of Bibliographies Relating to Mexican American Studies." *El Grito,* 3 (Summer, 1970), 25-31.
Lists 89 bibliographies published from 1928 through 1970. Currently being revised and expanded.

Fairbanks, Helen. *Collective Bargaining in Agriculture.* Selected References No. 148. Princeton University, Industrial Relations Section, August, 1969.

Farm Workers: A Selected Bibliography. Detroit: Wayne State University, Archives of Labor History and Urban Affairs, [August, 1972]. 6 pp.
Short, highly selective list of books and articles about farm workers, Cesar Chavez, and the United Farm Workers, designed primarily to meet the needs of elementary, junior high, and high school students.

Farmers' and Farm Laborers' Strikes and Riots in the United States, 1932-1935: List of References. Washington: Dept. of Agriculture, Agricultural Economics Bureau Library, 1935. 83 pp.

Flynn, Barbara, *et al. Chicano: A Selected Bibliography.* Riverside, Calif.: Riverside Public Library. 1971. 92 pp.
Lists materials in the Inland Library System, Riverside and San Bernadino counties: books, periodicals, newspapers, government publications, pamphlets, and audio-visual material.

Folsom, Josiah C. *Agricultural Labor in the United States, 1943-1952: Bibliography of Selected References.* Washington: U.S. Dept. of Agriculture Library, Library List 61, March, 1954.

———. *Migratory Agricultural Labor in the United States: Annotated Bibliography of Selected References.* Washington: U.S. Dept. of Agriculture Library, Library List 59, May, 1953. 64 pp.

Fujimoto, Isao and Jo Clare Schieffer. *Guide to Sources on Agricultural Labor.* Davis, Calif.: Dept. of Applied Behavioral Sciences, University of California, 1968. 42 pp. Revised and updated, 1969. 39 pp.
Approximately one-half of this volume is devoted to the mechanics of finding materials. It lists indices and guides, agencies and organizations, bibliographies, and ephemeral materials, as well as a selected, annotated bibliography. The bibliography contains sections on general agriculture, California agriculture, technology and mechanization, braceros, poverty, and the unionization of farm workers. Definitive annotations.

"Graduate Studies in American Agricultural History." *Agricultural History,* 41 (July, 1967), 275-312.
Bibliography of unpublished theses and dissertations. Section on agricultural wage labor.

Hall, Carl W. *Bibliography on Mechanization and Labor in Agriculture.* Special Paper No. 6. East Lansing: Rural Manpower Center, Michigan State University, 1968. 18pp.
Relationships between mechanization and labor.

Hervey, Jack L. and Garth Holmquist. *Rural Manpower: An Annotated Bibliography.* Special Paper No. 5. East Lansing: Rural Manpower Center, Michigan State University, 1968. 41 pp.

Hopper, Jean. *The Migratory Farm Worker: A Selected Bibliography.* Philadelphia: The Free Library of Philadelphia, 1967. 6 pp. Also in *ALA Library Service to Labor Newsletter,* 20(Fall, 1967), 5-8.

Library of Congress. Legislative Reference Service. *The Mexican Farm Labor Program: References, 1951-1965,* by Mary R. Heslet. Washington, June, 1965.

———. Legislative Reference Service. *Mexican-Americans and Mexicans in the United States Since 1945: Selected References,* by W.H. Gilbert. Washington, 1965.

———. Legislative Reference Service. *Migrant Labor Law and Relations: Selected References, 1960-1969.* Washington, 1969.

———. Legislative Reference Service. *Migratory Agricultural Labor: References to Books, Periodicals, and Films, 1959-1969,* by Katherine S. Warnell. Washington, June, 1969. 31 pp.
Sections on general references; bracero program; California grape strike; education; health, housing, and welfare; income; and films.

———. Legislative Reference Service. *Migratory Agricultural Labor: References to Federal Publications, Studies and Reports. 1959-1968.* by Mary R. Heslet, revised by Helen N. Grubbs. Washington, 1969. 12 pp.
Sections on congressional hearings, reports, and committee prints; departmental publications; the President's Committee on Migratory Labor; and U.S. treaties.

Meier, Matt S. "Dissertations," *Journal of Mexican American History.* 1(Spring, 1971). 170-190.
Bibliography of theses and dissertations, 1908-1970, on the history of the Mexican American. Includes a number of items pertaining to migrant labor and past attempts to organize farm workers.

Meier, Matt S. and Feliciano Rivera. *A Bibliography For Chicano History.* San Francisco: R and E Associates, 1972. 96 pp.
Chronological arrangement covering the period from colonial days to the present. Contains separate sections on labor and immigration, civil rights, Mexican American culture, theses and dissertations, and bibliographies.

Mexican-American Bibliography. Redlands, Calif.: University of Redlands, Armacost Library, Dept. of Special Collections, August, 1970. 14 pp.
Lists items in the Library.

Mexican-American Bibliography. Sacramento: Sacramento State College, Library, 1969.

Mexican-American History: A Critical Selective Bibliography. Santa Barbara, Calif.: Mexican-American Historical Society, 1969. Second edition in *Journal of Mexican American History.* 1(Fall, 1970), 69-86.

Major divisions are: 1. Background; 2. Mexican-American History, 1848-1970; and 3. Non-Historical Sources. This last section includes items pertaining to Cesar Chavez. UFWOC, and the grape strike.

Mexican-American Study Project Revised Bibliography. With a Bibliographical Essay by Ralph Guzman. Advance Report 3. Los Angeles: Division of Research, Graduate School of Business, University of California, 1967. 99 pp.

Devoted primarily to works pertaining to urban social and economic problems. Contains sections on books and pamphlets, general articles, education, rural migrant labor, government publications, dissertations, unpublished materials, and bibliographies. Partially annotated.

Migrant Farm Workers in the State of Washington: A Selected, Annotated Bibliography. Prepared for the Office of Economic Opportunity. Seattle: Consulting Services Corp., November, 1966. 50 pp.

Although primarily concerned with preparing materials for a study of migrants in Washington, it includes interrelated materials about migrants in other states, especially Texas and California. Contains sections on costs and revenues, education, employment, health, housing, legislation, mechanization, social characteristics, state and federal reports, bracero program, wages, and miscellaneous publications.

Navarro, Eliseo. *The Chicano Community: A Selected Bibliography For Use in Social Work Education.* New York: Council on Social Work Education, 1971. 57 pp.

Lists books, articles, government publications, reports, and proceedings. Definitive annotations.

Neufeld, Maurice F. *A Representative Bibliography of American Labor History.* Ithaca, N.Y.: Cornell University, School of Industrial and Labor Relations, 1964. 146 pp.

Covers a wide variety of types of materials, including fiction. Section on agriculture.

Nogales, Luis G., ed. *The Mexican American: A Selected and Annotated Bibliography.* Second edition, revised and enlarged. Stanford: Center for Latin American Studies, Stanford University, 1971. 162 pp.

Lists 444 books, pamphlets, reports, articles, dissertations and theses, bibliographies, and government documents. Also includes a listing of

Chicano periodicals. Highly selective, but thoroughly and definitively annotated.

Ohio. State Library. *The Migratory Farm Worker.* Selected Publication List No. 9. Columbus, 1968. 2 pp.

Revelle, Keith. *Chicano!: A Selected Bibliography of Materials By and About Mexico and Mexican Americans.* Oakland, Calif.: Oakland Public Library, Latin American Library, 1969. 21 pp.
Lists approximately 80 books, newspapers, periodicals, articles, reports, and speeches in the Latin American Library.

———. "A Collection for La Raza," *Library Journal,* 96 (November 15, 1971), 3719-3726.
Lists books, Spanish-language magazines and newspapers, the Chicano press, and audio-visual materials. Intended as an "aid to make Chicano materials more accessible to the librarian. . . ."

Ruesink, David C. and T. Brice Batson. *Bibliography Relating to Agricultural Labor.* Departmental Information Report No. 69-1. College Station, Texas: Dept. of Agricultural Economics and Sociology, Texas A & M University, 1969.

Schieffer, Jo Clare and Isao Fujimoto. *Social Implications of Agricultural Mechanization: A Bibliography.* Davis, Calif.: Dept. of Applied Behavioral Sciences, University of California, 1969. 43 pp.

Schlebecker, John T. *Bibliography of Books and Pamphlets on the History of Agriculture in the United States. 1607-1967.* Santa Barbara, Calif.: Clio Press, 1969. 183 pp.

Schramko, Linda Fowler. *Chicano Bibliography: Selected Materials on Americans of Mexican Descent.* Revised edition. Sacramento: Sacramento State College Library, 1970.
Lists holdings in the Sacramento State College Library.

Sheridan, George. *An Annotated Bibliography of Mexican American Education.* Los Angeles: Teacher Corps Rural-Migrant, School of Education, University of Southern California, 1971. vii + 28 pp.
"It is intended especially for those who teach . . . in the fifth through twelfth grades." Among the books and pamphlets listed are many dealing with Cesar Chavez, UFWOC, and farm labor. Also included are a number of sources not found in other bibliographies: museums, posters, music and theater, and sources in Mexico.

Shideler, James H. and Lawrence B. Lee. *A Preliminary List of References For the History of Agriculture in California.* Davis: Agricultural History Center, University of California, 1967. 62 pp.

Slobodek, Mitchell. *A Selective Bibliography of California Labor History.* Los Angeles: University of California, Institute of Industrial Relations, 1964. 265 pp.
Section on agriculture, pp. 17-34. Partially annotated.

U.S. Cabinet Committee on Opportunity For the Spanish Speaking. *The Spanish Speaking in the United States: A Guide to Materials.* Washington, 1971. 175 pp.
Revision and expansion of *A Guide to Materials Relating to Persons of Mexican Heritage in the United States,* a bibliography published in 1969 by the Committee's predecessor, the Inter-Agency Committee on Mexican American Affairs. Contains sections on bibliographies; books; articles, reports, and speeches; dissertations and other unpublished materials; government publications; and audio-visual materials. Also included are listings of U.S. producers and distributors of Spanish audio-visual materials, currently published periodicals, and Spanish-language radio and TV stations.

U.S. Dept. of Labor. Bureau of Labor Standards. *Selected References on Domestic Migratory Agricultural Workers. Their Families, Problems, and Programs, 1955-1960. Bulletin 225. Washington, June, 1961. 38 pp.*

———. Library. *Mexican Americans: Selected References.* Washington, February, 1967. 8 pp.

———. Office of Information. *Publications of the U.S. Department of Labor: Subject Listing, 1963 to June, 1968.* Washington, 1968. 74 pp.
Included are sections on agricultural labor and labor law.

Weber, Francis J. "A Bibliography of California Bibliographies," *Southern California Quarterly* [formerly, *Historical Society of Southern California Quarterly*], 50 (March, 1968), 5-32.
Useful for general reference works on California.

Yinger, Winthrop. "Cesar Chavez and *El Malcriado:* 1965-1970 Compilation," Fresno, Calif.: Institute for the Study of Contemporary Rhetoric, Fresno State College Library, September, 1970. 8 pp.
Listing of all references to Cesar Chavez appearing in *El Malcriado* (Delano: Farm Worker Press), issues No. 10 (1965) through August 15, 1970.

Government Documents

FEDERAL GOVERNMENT

U.S. Commission on Civil Rights

Hearing, San Antonio, Texas, December 9-14, 1968. Washington, 1969. 1304 pp.

Statements, testimony, and exhibits, including Commission Staff Reports: "Farm Workers" and "The Commuter on the United States—Mexico Border."

The Mexican American, by Helen Rowan. Washington, 1968. 69 pp.

Covers such subjects as civil rights and the administration of justice, education, employment, and public policies and agencies.

Mexican Americans and the Administration of Justice in the Southwest. Report of the Commission. Washington, 1970. 135 pp.

Sections on law enforcement, the judicial process, language, and participation by Mexican Americans in agencies of law enforcement and justice. Chapter on "Interference With Mexican American Organizational Efforts" refers to UFWOC problems with the Texas Rangers in Starr County, Texas.

Stranger In One's Land. Washington, May, 1970. 49 pp.

The stranger is the Mexican American. Chapters on language; green-card commuters and their effect upon the organizing efforts of domestic farm workers; poverty in the Rio Grande Valley of Texas; education; discrimination in employment; and legal discrimination, especially by the Texas Rangers.

U.S. Congress, House

Committee on Education and Labor. *Coverage of Agricultural Employees Under the National Labor Relations Act.* Hse. Rept. 1274. 90th Cong., 2nd Sess., 1968. 43 pp.

U.S. Congress, House Committee on Education and Labor (continued)
Majority and minority viewpoints and testimony on H.R. 16014. Includes statements by Cesar Chevez, Larry Itliong, Dolores Huerta, and Walter Reuther.

———. General Subcommittee on Labor. *Registration of Farm Labor Contractors.* Hearings on H.R. 5060. 88th Cong., 1st Sess., 1963. 150 pp.

———. Select Subcommittee on Labor. *Education of Migrant Agricultural Employees and Their Children.* Hearings on S. 1124. 87th Cong., 2nd Sess., 1962. 144 pp.
Includes statements by Selma Borchardt, James Vizzard, Steve Allen, Senator Harrison Williams, and Fay Bennett.

———. Select Subcommittee on Labor. *Migratory Labor.* Hearings on H.R. 5288-5291. 87th Cong., 1st Sess., 1961. 366 pp.
Bills relate to the registration of farm labor contractors, recruitment and transportation, and child labor.

———. Special Subcommittee on Labor. *Employment of "Green Card" Aliens During Labor Disputes.* Hearings on H.R. 12667, July 16-August 8, 1969. 91st Cong., 1st Sess., 1969. 250 pp.
Includes testimony and statements by Dolores Huerta, UFWOC vice-president; and William Kircher, AFL-CIO director of organization.

———. Special Subcommittee on Labor. *Extension of the National Labor Relations Act to Agricultural Employees.* Hearings on H.R. 4769. 90th Cong., 1st Sess., 1967. 294 pp. 2nd Sess., 1968. 30 pp.
Includes statements by Cesar Chavez, Dolores Huerta, Larry Itliong, Mack Lyons, Gilbert Padilla, Ronald Haughton, and Walter Reuther.

———. Subcommittee on Agricultural Labor. *Agricultural Child Labor Act of 1971.* Hearings on H.R. 10499 and H.R. 1597, Sept. 16-29, 1971. 92nd Cong., 1st Sess., 1971. 275 pp.

———. Subcommittee on Agricultural Labor. *Migrant Manpower Problems.* Hearings on Title III of H.R. 5010, June 30, 1971 and April 24, 1972. 92nd Cong., 2nd Sess., 1972. 339 pp.

———. Subcommittee on Agricultural Labor. *Seminar on Farm Labor Problems.* Hearings on H.R. 5010 and Related Bills: Public Regulation of Working Conditions in Agriculture, June 2, 3, and 10, 1971. 92nd Cong., 1st Sess., 1971. 246 pp.
Statements, reports, and papers, including "The History of the Farm Labor Movement in the 20th Century," by Daniel H. Pollitt, pp. 53-72.

———. Subcommittee on Agricultural Labor. *Workmen's Compensation For Farmworkers.* Hearings on H.R. 11007, October-November, 1971. 92nd Cong., 1st Sess., 1971. 153 pp.

———. Subcommittee on General Education. *Migrant Children Education.* Hearings on H.R. 9872 and H.R. 10378. 86th Cong., 2nd Sess., 1960. 215 pp.

Committee on Interstate and Foreign Commerce. Subcommittee on Public Health and Welfare. *Health Services For Migratory and Seasonal Agricultural Workers.* Hearings on H.R. 13432, Sept. 29, 1969. 91st Cong., 1st Sess., 1969. 39 pp.

U.S. Congress, Senate

Appropriations Committee. *Farm Labor in a Changing Agriculture.* Part 4 of Hearings on H.R. 10509. 90th Cong., 1st Sess., 1967. 94 pp.
Department of Agriculture report regarding labor shortages during peak harvest periods, listing California, Texas, Florida, New York, and Michigan as critical areas.

Committee on Labor and Public Welfare. *Migrant Farm Workers in America,* by D.H. Pollit and S.M. Levine. Committee Print. 86th Cong., 2nd Sess., 1960. 79 pp.

———. Subcommittee on Employment, Manpower, and Poverty. *Hunger and Malnutrition in the United States.* Hearings on S. Res. 281. 90th Cong., 2nd Sess., 1968. 479 pp.

———. Subcommittee on Health. *Migrant Health Services.* Hearings on S. 2660, October 21 and 22, 1969. 91st Cong., 1st Sess., 1969. 115 pp.

———. Subcommittee on Labor. *Agricultural Labor Legislation.* Hearings on S. 1808, April 16-June 18, 1969. 91st Cong., 1st Sess., 1969. 375 pp.
Includes statement submittted by Cesar Chavez, as well as testimony by Dolores Huerta and Jerome Cohen, April 16, 1969.

———. Subcommittee on Labor and Labor-Management Relations. *Migratory Labor.* Hearings. 82nd Cong., 2nd Sess., 1952. 2 Parts. 1089 pp.

———. Subcommittee on Migratory Labor. *Amending Migratory Labor Laws.* Hearings on S. 1864-1868, July, 1965 and March-April, 1966. 89th Cong., 1st and 2nd Sess., 1966. 838 pp.
Hearings in Sacramento, Delano, Visalia, Washington, and San Antonio on bills relating to minimum wage, child labor, collective bargaining rights, and recruitment and transportation. Includes testimony and statements of Cesar Chavez, Dolores Huerta, Wayne Hartmire, and Larry Itliong.

———. Subcommittee on Migratory Labor. *Farmworkers in Rural America, 1971-1972.* Hearings. 92nd Cong., 1st and 2nd Sess., 1971-1972. 3554 pp.
Part 1 "Farmworkers in Rural Poverty"
Part 2 "Who Owns the Land?"
Parts 3A-C "Land Ownership, Use, and Distribution"
Parts 4A-B "Role of Land-Grant Colleges"
Parts 5A-B "Appendix"

———. Subcommittee on Migratory Labor. *Migrant Health Program: Current Operations and Additional Needs.* Committee Print. 90th Cong., 1st Sess., 1967. 48 pp.

———. Subcommittee on Migratory Labor. *Migrant Health Services.* Hearings on S. 2688. 90th Cong., 1st Sess., 1967. 174 pp.

———. Subcommittee on Migratory Labor. *Migrant and Seasonal Farmworker Powerlessness.* Hearings. 91st Cong., 1st and 2nd Sess., 1969-1970. 8 parts. 6316 pp.
Part 1 "Who Are the Migrants?"
Part 2 "The Migrant Subculture"
Parts 3A-B "Efforts to Organize"

U.S. Congress, Senate, Committee on Labor and Public Welfare (continued)
Parts 4A-B "Farmworker Legal Problems"
Parts 5A-B "Border Commuter Labor Problem"
Parts 6A-C "Pesticides and the Farmerworker"
Parts 7A-B "Manpower and Economic Problems"
Parts 8A-C "Who Is Responsible?"

———. Subcommittee on Migratory Labor. *Migratory Farm Labor Problem in the United States.*
1965. 89th Cong., 1st Sess., S. Report 155. 77 pp.
1966. 89th Cong., 2nd Sess., S. Report 1549. 163 pp.
1967. 90th Cong., 1st. Sess., S. Report 71. 73 pp.
1968. 90th Cong., 2nd Sess., S. Report 1006. 100 pp.
1969. 91st Cong., 1st Sess., S. Report 83. 152 pp.

All of the Senate Reports, *Migratory Farm Labor Problem in the United States,* generally follow the same format. They include sections on "Background Facts, Legislative Accomplishments and Continuing Needs" (health, education, farm labor contractors, foreign workers under P.L. 78 and P.L. 414, housing, wages, child labor, sanitation, nutrition, OEO programs, and legal aid), and "Problems Calling For Basic Legislation" (collective bargaining, wages, unemployment insurance, child labor, workmens compensation, Social Secruity, transportation, residence requirements, voluntary farm employment service, foreign workers, tax amortization for housing, and establishment of a National Advisory Council on Migratory Labor). Also included are individual views of senators, notes, and appendices consisting of tables, charts, maps, statements, texts of laws, and other miscellaneous data. The 1966 Report (89th Cong., S. Report 1549) contains separate sections devoted to farm produce and income, wages, and food prices. Approximately two-thirds of this report consists of the views of Senator George Murphy.

———. Subcommittee on Migratory Labor. *Migratory Labor.* Hearings on S. 1085, S. 1778, S. 2141, and S. 2498. 86th Cong., 1st and 2nd Sess., 1959-1960. 2 parts. 1853 pp.
Bills pertain to minimum wage, registration of crew leaders and farm labor contractors, and child labor. Includes statements by Msgr. George Higgins, Allan Grant, Thomas McCullough, and Norman Smith.

———. Subcommittee on Migratory Labor. *Migratory Labor.* Hearings on S. 1123 and related bills. 87th Cong., 1st and 2nd Sess., 1961-1962. 3 volumes. 956 pp.
Bills relate to child labor, farm labor contractors, education, establishing a National Citizens Council on Migratory Labor, health, recruitment and transportation, and sanitation. Includes bibliography on migrant labor, pp. 85-124.

———. Subcommittee on Migratory Labor. *Migratory Labor Bills.* Hearings on S. 521-526. 88th Cong., 1st Sess., 1963. 313 pp.
Education, day-care, child labor, farm labor contractors, National Advisory Council on Migratory Labor, and sanitation.

U.S. Congress, Senate, Committee on Labor and Public Welfare (continued)
———. Subcommittee on Migratory Labor. *Migratory Labor Legislation.* Hearings on S. 8, S. 195, S. 197, and S. 198, May-September, 1967. 90th Cong., 1st Sess., 1967. 4 parts. 1018 pp.
Amending the NLRA, establishing a National Advisory Council on Migratory Labor, child labor, and recruitment and transportation. Hearings took place in Washington, D.C.; Rio Grande City and Edinburg, Texas; and Rochester, N.Y.

U.S. Department of Agriculture

Agricultural Research Service. *Housing For Migrant Agricultural Workers.* Washington, August, 1970. 43 pp.

Economic Research Service. *The Hired Farm Working Force of 1966: A Statistical Report,* by Robert C. McElroy. Agricultural Economic Report 120. Washington, September, 1967. 30 pp.
Reports are issued annually.

———. *A Socio-Economic Profile of the 1965 Farm Wage Force.* Agricultural Economic Report No. 157. Washington, April, 1969. 39 pp.

———. *Termination of the Bracero Program: Some Effects on Farm Labor and Migrant Housing Needs.* Agricultural Economic Report No. 77. Washington, June, 1965. 28 pp.
Includes brief history of the importation of braceros and the growth of agriculture in the United States

U.S. Department of Labor

Background Information on Farm Labor. Washington, March 19, 1965. [29] pp.
Contains separate articles relating primarily to the effects of the end of the bracero program.

Farm Labor Fact Book. Washington, 1959. 240 pp.
Chapters on the farm work force, farm operators, unpaid family workers, hired farm workers, migrant farm workers, imported farm workers, and wages and hours. Numerous tables and charts.

Final Report of the California Farm Labor Panel to Secretary of Labor W. Willard Wirtz, Los Angeles, December 1, 1965. 52 pp.

Final Report of the Michigan Farm Labor Panel to Secretary of Labor W. Willard Wirtz, Detroit, December 30, 1965. 45 pp.
How the pickle cucumber growers are going to manage with domestic workers instead of braceros.

Problems Involved in Applying a Federal Minimum Wage to Agricultural Workers, by Harry S. Kantor, et al. 2 vols. Washington, April 30, 1960. Vol. 1, 272 pp. Vol. 2, 253 pp.
Sections on the labor market, governmental action, and problems and issues. Second part is a statistical appendix.

Year of Transition: Seasonal Farm Labor, 1965. Report from the Secretary of Labor. Washington, 1966.
Transition from foreign labor to domestic labor necessitated by the termination of P.L. 78.

U.S. Department of Labor (Continued)

Bureau of Labor Standards. *Agricultural Workers and Workmen's Compensation*. Bulletin 206, revised. Washington, January, 1964. 19 pp.

———. *Child Workers in Agriculture*. Leaflet No. 4. Washington, 1959. 4 pp.

———. *Coverage of Agricultural Workers Under State and Federal Labor Laws*. Bulletin No. 264. Washington, 1964. 26 pp.

———. *Major Provisions of State and Federal Farm Contractors' Labor Laws*, by Deborah T. Bond. Bulletin No. 275. Washington, May, 1965. 21 pp.

———. *Status of Agricultural Workers Under State and Federal Labor Laws*. Fact Sheet No. 2. Washington, 1965. 16 pp.

Bureau of Labor Statistics. *Labor Unionism in American Agriculture*, by Stuart Jamieson. Bulletin No. 836. Washington, 1945. 457 pp.
Definitive study which "endeavors both to record the history of farm labor unions and strikes in the United States, and to analyze them functionally in time and place." Includes lists of agricultural labor unions and good notes and bibliography.

Wage and Hour and Public Contracts Divisions. *Hired Farmworkers: A Study of the Effects of the $1.00 Minimum Wage Under the Fair Labor Standards Act*. Washington, 1968. 46 pp. + 91 page appendix.

———. *Hired Farm Workers: A Study of the Effects of the $1.15 Minimum Wage Under the Fair Labor Standards Act*. Washington, 1969. 56 pp. + 70 page appendix.

———. *Hired Farm Workers: A Study to Evaluate the Feasibility of Extending the Minimum Wage Under the Fair Labor Standards Act*. Washington, 1966.

U.S. Inter-Agency Committee on Mexican American Affairs:

The Mexican American: A New Focus on Opportunity. Testimony Presented at the Cabinet Committee Hearings On Mexican American Affairs, El Paso, Texas, October 26-28, 1967. Washington, 1968. 253 pp.
Prepared statements and articles presented on a wide variety of topics: agriculture, labor, health, education, housing.

The President's Remarks at the Installation of Commissioner Vicente T. Ximenes and a Cabinet Report on the Mexican American Community. Washington, June 9, 1967.

U.S. Library of Congress:

Legislative Reference Service. *The Strike of the United Farm Workers Organizing Committee in Delano, California: Background and Its Relationship to Legislative Efforts to Organize Farm Workers*. Washington, 1968.

U.S. President's Commission on Migratory Labor:

Migratory Labor in American Agriculture. Washington, 1951. 188 pp.
Discusses such topics as alien contract labor, illegal aliens, labor relations and collective bargaining, wages, housing, health and safety, education, and child labor.

U.S. President's Committee on Migratory Labor:

Report to the President on Domestic Migratory Labor. Washington, 1956. Second Report, 1960. 33 pp.
Includes sections on joint federal-state action, employment and income, housing, transportation, education, public health, public welfare, Social Security, reducing the need for migrancy, research, and programs in development.

U.S. President's National Advisory Commission on Rural Poverty:

The People Left Behind. Washington, September, 1967. 160 pp.
Includes the Commission's recommendations.

Rural Poverty. Hearings, Memphis, Tucson, and Washington, D.C., January-February, 1967. Washington, 1967.

Rural Poverty in the United States. Washington, May, 1968. 601 pp.
Thirty-two background papers written for the Commission by different authors, including "Hired Farm Labor in the West" by Varden Fuller, and "Migratory Agricultural Workers in the Eastern Seaboard States" by Olaf F. Larson.

U.S. Select Commission on Western Hemisphere Immigration:

The Impact of Commuter Aliens Along the Mexican and Canadian Borders. Hearings, January-March, 1968. 4 parts.
"Green-card" commuters. Hearings took place in El Paso, San Diego, Brownsville, and Detroit.

Report of the Commission, January, 1968. 197 pp.
Includes section on "commuters."

STATE GOVERNMENTS

Arizona

State Employment Service. Farm Placement Division. *Arizona Post-Season Farm Labor Report.* Phoenix, issued annually.

California

Advisory Committee on Farm Labor Research. *The California Farm Labor Force: A Profile.* Report, prepared for the Assembly Committee on Agriculture. [Sacramento]. April, 1969. 154 pp.
Includes a general profile of California farm labor, and special studies of migrants, Mexicans, students, income supplements, and housing as they relate to California farm labor. Numerous tables, charts, and statistics.

Agricultural Labor Commission. *Report and Recommendations of the Agricultural Labor Commission.* Sacramento, January, 1963. 471 pp.
Commission consisted of representatives from government, unions, and growers. Report includes findings and recommendations, minutes, hearing transcripts, and exhibits.

Division of Farm Labor Service. *California Farm Labor Report.* Sacramento, issued annually.

Legislature. Assembly. *The Bracero Program and Its Aftermath: An Historical Summary.* Sacramento, April 1, 1965. 23 pp.

———. Assembly. Committee on Agriculture. *California Farm Labor Survey.* Progress Report 621. Sacramento, 1968.

———. Assembly. Committee on Agriculture. *Pesticides and Worker Laws.* Interim hearings, November 23, December 9-10, 1970. Sacramento, 1970. 118 pp.

———. Senate. Fact Finding Committee on Agriculture. *Farm Labor Disputes: Special Report.* Sacramento, 1967. 31 pp.

———. Senate. Fact-Finding Committee on Labor and Welfare. *California's Farm Labor Problems.* Part 1. Sacramento, 1961. 326 pp. Part 2, 1963. 127 pp.
Cobey Committee. Part 1 consists of background and history of California's farm labor problems, mentioning possible solutions. Topics include labor supply and demand, foreign workers, wages, child labor, and unionization. Part 2 discusses agricultural labor disputes, minimum wage, housing, unemployment insurance, medical care, education, transportation, and safety. Both parts include statistical data.

———. Senate. Fact-Finding Subcommittee on Un-American Activities. *14th Report on Un-American Activities.* Sacramento, 1967. 209 pp.
"The purpose of this report is to submit information pertaining to the degree of subversive impact in the Delano grape strike."

Office of Economic Opportunity. *California Migrant Master Plan.* Second Progress Report. Sacramento, 1967.

Michigan

Civil Rights Commission. *A Field Study of Migrant Workers in Michigan: Report and Recommendations.* Detroit, 1969. 20 pp.
Essentially a follow-up study of the 1968 *Report and Recommendations* of the Commission.

———. *Problems of Migrant Workers in Michigan,* by Roy O. Fuentes. Staff Report of the Northern Michigan Region, Michigan Civil Rights Commission, March, 1968. 12 pp.

———. *Report and Recommendations On the Status of Migratory Farm Labor in Michigan.* Detroit, 1968. 24 pp.
Gives basic summary of problems in the areas of employment, housing, education, health, social services, community attitude, and federal government responsibility. Based on interviews with laborers and growers and on public hearings.

Department of Education. Bureau of Library Services. "A Better Day For Michigan Migrants," *Michigan in Books,* Vol. 10, No. 4 (Summer, 1969).

Department of Labor. Commission on Agricultural Labor. [First] *Annual Report '70.* Lansing, 1970.

Farm Labor Service Section. *Post Season Farm Labor Report.* Detroit, issued annually.

Governor's Task Force on Migrant Labor: Final Report. [Lansing], October, 1969. 28 pp.

Report of the Governor's Commission on Migrant Labor. Lansing, 1965. 25 pp.

Second Report of the Governor's Commission on Migrant Labor. Lansing, 1966. 28 pp.

Ohio

Department of Industrial Relations. *Migratory Labor in Ohio Agriculture.* Columbus, 1966.

Pennsylvania

Governor's Committee on Migratory Labor. *Pennsylvania Migratory Labor Report.* June, 1970. 33 pp.

Texas

Bureau of Labor Statistics. *Report on Migratory Labor Movement and Licensed Labor Agents,* issued annually.

Texas [Continued]

Good Neighbor Commission. *Texas Migrant Labor: The Migration.* Austin, issued annually.

Wisconsin

Equal Rights Commission. *State and Federal Rights of Migrant Farm Workers: An Appraisal,* by Mark Erenburg. Madison, 1967. 22 pp.

Theses and Dissertations, Annual Reports, Proceedings, and Unpublished Materials

Bennett, Fay. *The Condition of Farm Workers and Small Farmers in 1969.* Report to the National Board of the National Sharecroppers Fund. Washington, D.C., 1969. 5 pp.

This report, as well as the reports for previous years, contains sections on the organization of farm workers, legislation, living and working conditions, government programs, mechanization, the decline of the small farmer, and pesticides. For 1970 and 1971 reports, *see* listing under James Pierce.

Briegel, Kaye. "The History of Political Organizations Among Mexican Americans in Los Angeles Since the Second World War." Master's thesis, University of Southern California, 1967.

Brown, Jerald Barry. "The United Farm Workers Grape Strike and Boycott, 1965-1970: An Evaluation of the Culture of Poverty Theory." Ph.D. dissertation, Cornell University, 1972. 348 pp.

Discusses agribusiness; the table grape industry; the history of agricultural unionization in California; the grape strike and boycott; and the leadership, membership, and organizational structure of UFWOC.

Buschlen, M.J. "Growers Must Know How to Handle Labor Confrontations." Michigan State Horticultural Society, *100th Annual Report, 1970,* pp. 40-45.

"Growers in Michigan still have time to study U.F.W.O.C. contracts which have been signed, before next harvest season."

———. "Potential Seasonal Labor Problems Confronting Michigan Fruit Growers." Michigan State Horticultural Society, *99th Annual Report, 1969,* pp. 51-57.

"The most obvious problems involve strikes, walkouts, slowdowns, boycotts and violence."

Clark, Douglas M. "Wheatland Hop Field Riot." Master's thesis, Chico [California] State College, 1963.

Daniel, Franz. "Problems of Union Organization for Migratory Workers." *Proceedings* of the Spring Meeting of the Industrial Relations Research Assn., May 4-5, 1961. Reprinted in *Labor Law Journal,* 12 (July, 1961), pp. 636-643.

Drake, Jim. "The Farm Worker," in *A Pride of Lions: America's Cultural Communities and the Preparation of Teachers.* Report on the Fourth National Conference of the U.S. Office of Education Tri-University Project in Elementary Education. Minneapolis, September 19-20, 1968, pp. 180-205.

NFWA, Chavez, education for migrant children.

Eisenman, Jerome. "Unrest in American Agriculture, 1941-1951, With Special Reference to California." Master's thesis, University of California at Berkeley, 1962, 261 pp.

Elac, John Chala. "The Employment of Mexican Workers in U.S. Agriculture, 1900-1960: A Binational Economic Analysis." Ph.D. dissertation, University of California at Los Angeles, 1961.

Gallardo, Lloyd L. "An Evaluation of United States Department of Labor Policy Regarding Wages Paid Mexican Nationals: Michigan Pickles, A Case Study." Ph.D. dissertation, University of California at Berkeley, 1962. 252 pp.

Georgi, Peter Hugh. "The Delano Grape Strike and Boycott: Inroads to Collective Bargaining in Agriculture." Senior thesis, Massachusetts Institute of Technology, August, 1969. vi + 134 pp. Reprinted in U.S. Senate Subcommittee on Migratory Labor, *Migrant and Seasonal Farmworker Powerlessness,* Part 3A.
Contains chapters on the history of California farm labor, Federal and State legislation, agribusiness and the grower's case, the strike and boycott, and negotiations. Good notes and bibliography.

Giumarra, John G., Jr. "The Produce Industry and Unionization." Address delivered to the International Apple Association, 74th Convention, Philadelphia, November 11, 1968.

Glass, Judith Chanin. "Conditions Which Facilitate Unionization of Agricultural Workers: A Case Study of the Salinas Valley Lettuce Industry." Ph.D. dissertation, University of California at Los Angeles, 1966.

Graves, Elaine F. "*El Malcriado* Anthology, 1965-1972." Master's thesis, Fairfield [Connecticut] University, 1973.

Halcomb, Ellen L. "Efforts to Organize the Migrant Workers By the Cannery and Agricultural Workers." Master's thesis, Chico [California] State College, 1963.

Hough, John. "Agricultural Labor Relations in the Imperial Valley From 1928 to 1934." Master's thesis, University of Southern California, 1951.

Hulpke, John F. "The Position of California Labor in Regard to the Bracero Program, 1942-1962." Master's thesis, San Francisco State College, 1963.

Industrial Relations Research Association. *Proceedings of Twenty-third Annual Winter Meeting,* December 28-29, 1970. Part 2, "Problems of Migrant Workers," pp. 11-32.
Consists of "Migratory Labor: A Review of Labor Market Problems," by Mark Erenburg; "Empirical Studies Bearing on the Market For Migratory Farm Labor: Current Status and Requirements," by Herrington J. Bryce; and "Discussion," by Boren Chertkov.

Jeffs, William George. "The Roots of the Delano Grape Strike." Master's thesis, California State College at Fullerton, June, 1969. 157 pp.
"The power which the growers have held for almost a century has been effectively confronted by the power of an organized minority segment of society." Includes discussion of agribusiness and small farmers, community organizing, labor contractors, foreign labor, previous attempts at unionization, and the origins of UFWOC.

Jones, Lamar B. "Mexican-American Labor Problems in Texas." Ph.D. dissertation, University of Texas, Austin, 1965. 244 pp.

Kuhrt, William J. "The California Boycott and Its Implications to American Agriculture." New York State Horticultural Society *Proceedings*, 114 (1969).

Landolt, Robert G. "The Mexican American Workers of San Antonio, Texas." Ph.D. dissertation, University of Texas, Austin, 1965.

Levine, Louis. "The Migratory Worker in the Farm Economy." *Proceedings* of the Spring Meeting of the Industrial Relations Research Association, May 4-5, 1961. Reprinted in *Labor Law Journal*, 12 (July, 1961), pp. 622-630.

Lowenstein, Norman. "Strikes and Strike Tactics in California Agriculture." Master's thesis, University of California at Berkeley, 1940.

McNamara, Patrick H. "Bishops, Priests and Prophecy: A Study in the Sociology of Protest." Ph.D. dissertation, University of California at Los Angeles, 1968. 205 pp.
". . . priests who began by ministering pastorally to Mexican-American migratory agricultural workers, gradually came to take a protesting stance against social injustices they perceived in the entire migratory labor system in the American Southwest."

Meister, Richard T. "Crisis in Agricultural Communications," Michigan State Horticultural Society, *100th Annual Report, 1970*, pp. 45-52.
Discusses the growers' need for better public relations to present their viewpoints regarding pesticides and unionization.

Mitchell, H. L. "Protest As a Means of Social Change." Address to the Department of History, University of Indiana at Fort Wayne, December 10, 1969. 6 pp.
Author is co-founder of the Southern Tenant Farmers Union, which he sees as the forerunner of UFWOC.

The New Farm Worker, U.S.A. Report of the National Executive Board to the 17th Convention, National Farm Labor Union. Memphis, Tennessee, December 8-9, 1951. 18 pp.
Corporate farms, organizing farm workers in California and the South,

importation of Mexican Nationals, farm labor legislation, and the President's Commission on Migratory Labor.

Palmer, Lane. "Your New Specialty Is People," Address to the National Association of County Agriculture Agents, Corvallis, Oregon, August 18, 1970. Reprinted in Michigan State Horticultural Society, *100th Annual Report, 1970,* pp. 151-158.
"We must do everything we can to get our story [regarding pesticides and farm labor] across to the public and correct the many misconceptions they hold."

Peters, James Preston. "Agricultural Unionism in the Imperial Valley, 1928-1940." Master's thesis, University of California at San Diego, 1967.

Pierce, James M. *The Condition of Farm Workers and Small Farmers in 1971.* Report to the National Board of the National Sharecroppers Fund. New York, 1971. 12 pp.
See listing under Fay Bennett.

Salandini, Victor. "The Short-Run Socio-Economic Effects of the Termination of Public Law 78 On the California Farm Labor Market For 1965-1967." Ph.D. dissertation, Catholic University, 1969. 300 pp.

Schmidt, Fred H. "Rationalizing the Farm Labor Market: The Case For Supplemental Wage Payments." Southwestern Social Science Assn., Economics Section, Annual Meeting, April 16, 1965. 21 pp. + 4 pp.

Schwartz, Harry. "Unionization of Agricultural Labor in the United States." Master's thesis, Columbia University, 1941.

Tangri, Beverly Starika. "Federal Legislation As an Expression of United States Public Policy Toward Agricutural Labor, 1914-1954." Ph.D. dissertation, University of California at Berkeley, 1967. 530 pp
Federal legislation has exhibited a policy based on the needs of the grower. Congress has passed legislation to increase the supply of labor but consistently neglected the workers, exempting agricultural labor from the Social Security Act, NLRA, and Fair Labor Standards Act.

Thompson, Mark E. "The Agricultural Workers Organizing Committee, 1959-1962." Master's thesis, Cornell University, 1963. 197 pp.

Unidos—Organizing For Local Action: Statewide Conference Concerning Farm Workers. Lansing: Michigan Catholic Conference, March 8, 1969. 55 pp.

United Automobile Workers. *Proceedings of the Constitutional Convention.* 19th-23rd Conventions, 1964-1972, 5 vols.
Contains various references to the United Farm Workers, the grape strike

and boycotts, and the financial and moral support given to UFWOC by the UAW.

Vito, James C. "An Analysis of Farm Labor Problems in California." Master's thesis, San Jose State College, 1968. 90 pp.

Washington State Horticultural Association. *Proceedings*, 65th Annual Meeting, 1969.
Includes a number of papers on agricultural labor, housing, lobbying, legislation, the fruit industry, and mechanization.

Williams, Harrison A., Jr. "Proposed Legislation For Migratory Workers." *Proceedings* of the Spring Meeting of the Industrial Relations Research Assn., May 4-5, 1961. Reprinted in *Labor Law Journal*, 12 (July, 1961), pp. 630-636.

Wilson, Ione Elizabeth. "The IWW in California, With Special Reference to Migratory Labor, 1910-1913." Master's thesis, University of California at Berkeley, 1946.

Winn, Charles Carr. "The Valley Farm Workers Movement, 1966-1967." Master's thesis, University of Texas at Arlington, 1970. 108 pp.
Lower Rio Grande Valley in Texas.

Woods, Cameron E. "Mexican Agricultural Labor in California." Master's thesis, Fresno State College, 1950.

Zuckerman, John. "Labor Unions and Seasonal Labor," Oregon State Horticultural Society, 52nd *Annual Report*, 1960, pp. 119-122.
Urges resistance to efforts to unionize farm labor in California.

Books and Pamphlets

Acuna, Rodolfo. *Occupied America: The Chicano's Struggle Toward Liberation.* New York: Canfield Press, 1972. 282 pp.
Chapter 7, "The Road to Delano," discusses UFWOC and previous attempts to organize farm workers.

Allen, Steve. *The Ground Is Our Table.* New York: Doubleday, 1966. Chapter 11, "Delano," gives the background of the grape strike and brief summary of past attempts at organizing farm workers.

American Friends Service Committee. *Child Labor in Agriculture, Summer, 1970: A Special Report.* Philadelphia. 1971. 110 pp.
Based upon studies of Washington, Oregon, Ohio, California, and Maine.

Anderson, Henry. *Fields of Bondage: The Mexican Contract Labor System in Industrialized Agriculture.* Berkeley, Calif., May 1, 1963. 104 pp.

———. *A Harvest of Loneliness.* Berkeley, Calif., 1964.

Auerbach, Jerold S. *Labor and Liberty: The LaFollette Committee and the New Deal.* Indianapolis: Bobbs-Merrill Co., 1966. 246 pp.
LaFollette Civil Liberties Committee, 1936-1940. Chapter 8, "The Committee and Farm Factories," discusses investigation of agricultural labor practices in California. Good chapter references and general bibliography.

Barnes, Robert F. *The California Migrant Farm Worker, His Family, and the Rural Community.* Research Monograph No. 6. Davis, Calif.: Department of Applied Behavioral Sciences, University of California, 1967. 41 pp.

Basta! The Tale of Our Struggle. Delano, Calif.: Farm Worker Press, 1966. 73 pp.
Photographs of the early days of the grape strike, including the Pilgrimage to Sacramento. Text and captions from the "Plan of Delano."

Bergan, Frank and Murray Norris. *Delano—Another Crisis for the Catholic Church.* Fresno, Calif.: Rudell Publishing Co., 1968.
Anti-UFWOC.

Berger, Samuel R. *Dollar Harvest: The Story of the Farm Bureau.* Foreword by Cesar Chavez. Lexington, Mass.: D.C. Heath and Co., 1971. 221 pp.

Bergez, John. "The Grape Strike in Delano: A Three-Part Case Study of Labor Problems in California Agriculture," in George E. Frakes and Curtis B. Solberg, *Minorities in California History.* New York: Random House, 1971, pp. 269-273.
Originally a three part article in *El Gaucho,* the student newspaper of the University of California at Santa Barbara, May 6-8, 1969.

Bergtholdt. Chris D. *A Different Look At Farm Labor Ideas.* Yuba City, Calif.: privately printed, [1965]. 10 pp.
Written by a retired farmer and directed to farm operators: "So as crazy as the idea seems, if agricultural producers want freedom in labor relations, they had better begin doing something to help farm laborers organize."

Briegel, Kaye. "The Development of Mexican American Organizations," in Manuel P. Servin, *The Mexican-Americans: An Awakening Minority.* Beverly Hills. Calif.: Glencoe Press, 1970, pp. 160-178.
Includes information on Chavez, Community Service Organization, NFWA, and attempts to unionize farm workers in the late 1920's.

Burma, John H., ed. *Mexican-Americans in the United States: A Reader.* Cambridge, Mass.: Schenkman Publishing Co., 1970. 487 pp.
Anthology of articles, scholarly studies, and essays on a wide variety of topics.

Bustamante, Charles J. and Patricia L. Bustamante. *The Mexican-American and the United States.* Mountain View, Calif.: PATTY-LAR Publications, 1969. 60 pp.
Includes information on Community Service Organization, Cesar Chavez, and organizing farm workers.

Cargill, B.F. and G.E. Rossmiller, eds. *Fruit and Vegetable Harvest Mechanization: Manpower Implications.* Report 17. East Lansing: Rural Manpower Center, Michigan State University, 1969.

Chambers, Clarke A. *California Farm Organizations: A Historical Study of the Grange, the Farm Bureau, and the Associated Farmers, 1929-1941.* Berkeley: University of California Press, 1952. 277 pp.
The activities of the organizations and their opposition to farm labor organizing.

Chavez, Cesar and Bayard Rustin. *Right To Work Laws—A Trap For America's Minorities.* New York: A. Philip Randolph Institute, n.d. 20 pp.
In English and Spanish.

Coles, Robert. *Uprooted Children: The Early Life of Migrant Farm Workers.* Pittsburgh: University of Pittsburgh Press, 1970. 142 pp.

Conklin, Melvin J. and Robert J. McElroy. *A Survey of Migrant Farmworker Housing in Oregon.* Station Bulletin 602. Corvallis, Ore.: Oregon State University, Agricultural Experiment Station, June, 1966. 39 pp.

Craig, Richard B. *The Bracero Program: Interest Groups and Foreign Policy.* Austin: University of Texas Press, 1971. 233 pp.

Day, Mark. *Forty Acres: Cesar Chavez and the Farm Workers.* Introduction by Cesar Chavez. New York: Praeger, 1971. 222 pp.
Primarily a narrative of Fr. Day's observations and experiences with UF-WOC from 1967 through 1970. In addition to descriptions of the various aspects and events of the strike from its origins in 1965 to the signing of contracts and the jail sentence of Chavez in 1970, *Forty Acres* also includes information on the background and growth of agribusiness; importation of farm workers; previous farm labor strikes; the role of the clergy; the Bishops Committee on Farm Labor Disputes; Filipino retirement village; Chavez's views on nonviolence; James Caswell; John Tunney; Bishop Patrick Flores; and the city of Delano.

The Delano Grape Story . . . From the Growers' View. Delano, Calif.: South Central Farmers Committee, July, 1968. 14 pp.

DeLeon, Nephtali. *Chicanos: Our Background and Our Pride.* Lubbock, Texas: Trucha Publications, 1972. 95 pp.
Chapter, "A Modern Prince of Peace," discusses Cesar Chavez and UF-WOC.

deToledano, Ralph. *Little Cesar.* New York: Anthem Press, 1971. 144 pp.
Highly critical of Cesar Chavez and UFWOC.

A Dialogue With Congress. Washington: National Campaign For Agricultural Democracy, 1969. 30 pp. + 3 pp. appendix.
Transcript of public hearing with Cesar Chavez and other UFWOC representatives before members of the U.S. House of Representatives, October 1, 1969, with Rep. James G. O'Hara presiding. Includes statements of Chavez, Andy Imutan, Mack Lyons, and Jerome Cohen, as well as questions put to Mr. Chavez by various congressmen.

Draper, Anne and Hal Draper. *The Dirt on California: Agribusiness and the University.* Berkeley, Calif.: The Independent Socialist Clubs of America, 1968. 32 pp.

Dunne, John Gregory. *Delano: The Story of the California Grape Strike.* New York: Farrar, Straus & Giroux, 1967. 176 pp. Revised and updated, 1971. 202 pp. Available in paperback, Noonday Press.
Cesar Chavez, NFWA, and the early days of the Delano grape strike. The additional chapter in the revised edition is titled "1971" and is an elaboration of Dunne's article, "To Die Standing," *Atlantic*, June, 1971.

Farm Workers and the Law: A Report on the Illegal Treatment of Farm Workers in California. Pasadena, Calif.: American Friends Service Committee, Farm Workers Opportunity Project, 1967. 62 pp.

Fineberg, Richard A. *Braceros By Any Other Name: Mexican Green Card Workers and Their Effect on U.S. Farm Labor.* Santa Barbara: McNally and Loftin, 1971.

———. *Green Card Labor and the Delano Grape Strike: A Study of Post-Bracero Mexican National Farm Workers in the San Joaquin Valley, 1968.* Claremont, Calif.: Council for Christian Action and Board for Homeland Ministries, United Church of Christ, 1968. [33] pp.

Fisher, Lloyd H. *The Harvest Labor Market in California.* Cambridge, Mass.: Harvard University Press, 1953. 183 pp.
Discusses organized labor, farm labor contractors, wage-fixing, and the importation of foreign farm workers.

Fishlow, David M., ed. *Sons of Zapata: A Brief Photographic History of the Farm Workers Strike in Texas.* Rio Grande City, Texas: United Farm Workers Organizing Committee, 1967.
Photographs and text.

Fitch, Bob. *My Eyes Have Seen.* San Francisco: Glide Publications, 1972.
Photographic essays on Cesar Chavez, Martin Luther King, Pete Seeger, Dorothy Day, the Berrigans, Ron Dellums, and Joan Baez.

——— and Lynne Fitch. *Soy Chicano: I Am Mexican-American.* Mankato, Minn.: Creative Educational Society, 1971. 64 pp.
Photographic essay told in the words of a thirteen-year old California girl who describes her life and her family, including their experiences in the grape strike and their activities with UFWOC.

Fogel, Walter. *Mexican-Americans in Southwest Labor Markets.* Advance Report No. 10, Mexican-American Study Project. Graduate School of Business, University of California at Los Angeles, 1967. 222 pp.

Foner, Philip S. *History of the Labor Movement in the United States.* Vol. 4, *The Industrial Workers of the World, 1905-1917.* New York: International Publishers, 1965.
Chapter 11, "Migratory Farm Workers: The Wheatland Affair," describes the strike in the hop fields, 1913. Chapter 21, "The Agricultural Workers Organization."

Franchere, Ruth. *Cesar Chavez.* New York: Crowell, 1970. 42 pp.
Children's book, kindergarten through grade three.

Friedland, William H. and Dorothy Nelkin. *Migrant: Agricultural Workers in America's Northeast.* New York: Holt, Rinehart and Winston, 1971. 281 pp.

Fuller, Varden. *No Work Today! The Plight of America's Migrants.* Public Affairs Pamphlet No. 190. New York: Public Affairs Committee, 1953. 28 pp.

Fusco, Paul and George D. Horowitz. *La Causa: The California Grape Strike.* New York: Collier Books, 1970. 158 pp.
Photographs and text giving the history of the grape strike and background on some of the participants. Extensive interviews with four strikers.

Galarza, Ernesto. *Merchants of Labor; The Mexican Bracero Story: An Account of the Managed Migration of Farm Workers in California, 1942-1960.* Santa Barbara: McNally & Loftin, 1964. 284 pp.

———. *Spiders in the House and Workers in the Field.* South Bend: University of Notre Dame Press, 1970. Available in paperback.
Primarily about the strike which began against DiGiorgio October 1, 1947, and the subsequent lawsuits and congressional action regarding the showing of the film, *Poverty In the Valley of Plenty,* including the Nixon-Morton-Steed investigation. Also contains background information on the DiGiorgio family. Describes "the decade-long effort of the National Agricultural Workers Union to organize farm labor and the spider-like intrigues which frustrated it. . . . It is the pre-Chavez, pre-Delano phase of the story."—Carey McWilliams, "Foreword."

———. *Strangers In Our Fields.* Washington: United States Section, Joint United States-Mexico Trade Union Committee, 1956. 80 pp.
Bracero program; violation by employers of laws designed to protect the rights of braceros.

———, Herman Gallegos, and Julian Samora. Photographs by George Ballis. *Mexican-American in the Southwest.* Santa Barbara: McNally and Loftin, 1969. 94 pp.
". . . surveys the effects of farm mechanization, urban redevelopment, population squeeze, and other root causes of upheaval . . ." Originally a report submitted to the Ford Foundation in 1966.

Gallego, Jose J. *Justicia al Obrero del Campo!* Chicago: Fabet Press Service, 1967. 40 pp.
Farm workers' strikes in California and Texas, Cesar Chavez, NWFA, Pilgrimage to Sacramento, "Plan of Delano," March to Austin.

Gentry, Curt. *The Last Days of the Late Great State of California.* New York: Ballantine Books, 1969.
Part 2, "The Central Valley," devoted to Cesar Chavez and UFWOC.

Grant, Allan and Murray Norris. *Clergy Views of Delano and the Grape Boycott.* Fresno, Calif.: Rudell Publishing Co.

Grebler, Leo, Joan W. Moore, and Ralph C. Guzman. *The Mexican-American People: The Nation's Second Largest Minority.* New York: The Free Press, 1970. 777 pp.
Primarily an urban sociological study but contains references to Chavez, the Delano grape strike, Rio Grande Valley strike, Migrant Ministry, the roles of various churches, and the unionization of farm workers. Extensive notes and bibliography.

Grubbs, Donald H. *Cry From the Cotton: The Southern Tenant Farmers' Union and the New Deal.* Chapel Hill: University of North Carolina Press, 1971. 218 pp.

Hadden, Jeffrey K. *The Gathering Storm in the Churches.* Garden City, N.Y.: Doubleday, 1969. 257 pp.
Reference to California Migrant Ministry and its involvement in the Delano grape strike, pp. 183-185.

Hartmire, Wayne C., Jr. *The Church and the Delano Grape Strike—A Partial Report.* Los Angeles: California Migrant Ministry, February, 1966. 10 pp.
Basic summary of facts and issues: origins and chronology of the strike, its leaders, and the role of the Migrant Ministry.

———. *The Church and the Emerging Farm Workers Movement.* Los Angeles: California Migrant Ministry, July 22, 1967. 40 pp. + vii.
Sections on agribusiness, the Delano strike and NFWA, the role of the Church in the strike, worker-priest programs, and nonviolence.

———. *Citizenship Education & Action in Tulare County.* Los Angeles: California Migrant Ministry, November 12, 1965. 12 pp.
Community development under the auspices of the California Migrant Ministry and the United Church of Christ. Discusses or refers to Mexican American Political Association (MAPA); Farm Workers Organization of Tulare County and its merger with NFWA; rent strike against Tulare County Housing Authority; grape strike; community reaction; AWOC; and California Agricultural Workers Union.

———. *The Delano Grape Strike: The Farm Workers' Struggle For Self-Determination.* Los Angeles: California Migrant Ministry, February, 1969. 6 pp.
Rebuttal of Allan Grant's article, "California Grapes and the Boycott: The Growers' Side of the Story."

Healy, Cletus. *Battle For the Vineyards.* New York: Twin Circle Publishing, 1969. 51 pp.
Anti-UFWOC. Compilation of articles originally in *Twin Circle* Magazine.

Heaps, Willard A. *Wandering Workers: The Story of American Migrant Farm Workers and Their Problems.* New York: Crown Publishers, 1968. 192 pp.
Written for "young adult" readers. Gives concise picture of living and working conditions throughout the country. Mentions Cesar Chavez, UF-WOC, and the grape strike.

Hightower, Jim. *Hard Tomatoes, Hard Times: The Failure of the Land Grant College Complex.* Preliminary Report of the Task Force on the Land Grant College Complex. Washington: Agribusiness Accountability Project, 1972. 308 pp.
Land grant colleges generally operate for the benefit of agribusiness while ignoring the problems of the small farmer, the farm worker, and the rural community.

Hill, Herbert. *No Harvest For the Reaper: The Story of the Migratory Agricultural Worker in the U.S.* New York: NAACP, 1960. 48 pp.

Hunsinger, George. *Notes On Delano: "The Hunsinger Report."* Fresno, Calif.: Valley Ministers' Association, 1967. 48 pp.

Jacobs, Paul. *The State of the Unions.* New York: Atheneum, 1963.
"The Forgotten People": P.L. 78, braceros, Teamsters, general information on migrant labor in the U.S. "A Matter of Spirit": 1961 AWOC, decrease in support from AFL-CIO International.

Koch, William H., Jr. *Dignity of Their Own: Helping the Disadvantaged Become First Class Citizens.* New York: Friendship Press, 1966. 190 pp.
Describes efforts to help migrants toward a better status. Projects of the Migrant Citizenship Education Project (under a grant from the Migrant Ministry). Case studies from Texas, Michigan, and Illinois.

Kostyu, Frank A. *Shadows in the Valley: The Story of One Man's Struggle For Justice.* New York: Doubleday, 1970. 192 pp.
Primarily about the Rev. Ed Krueger, the Texas Migrant Ministry, and Texas migrant workers. Contains a lengthy discussion of Cesar Chavez and the California grape strike.

Lamb, Ruth S. *Mexican Americans: Sons of the Southwest.* Claremont, Calif.: Ocelot Press, 1970. 198 pp.
Contains references to Cesar Chavez, UFWOC, and farm labor. Lengthy bibliography.

League For Industrial Democracy and National Sharecroppers Fund. *Down on the Farm: The Plight of Agricultural Labor.* New York, 1955. 14 pp.
Agribusiness, wages, living and working conditions, legislation, and attempts at unionization.

League of Women Voters. *The Migrant Workers.* Publication No. 328. Washington, December, 1967. 4 pp.

Leonard, Olen E. *Changes in the Spanish Speaking Labor Force of Saginaw County, Michigan.* State College, Social Science Research Center, Mississippi State University, 1968. 44 pp.

Let Justice Roll Down: Ethical Issues in the Relations Between Growers and Seasonal Workers in Industrialized Agriculture. New York: Migrant Ministry, National Council of Churches, March 14, 1963. Revised, March 15, 1968.
Chapters discuss definition of terms (*industrialized farm, family-like farm, grower, seasonal farm worker*), the economic situation, the policy positions of the National Council of Churches, and a summary of the ethical issues.

Lewis, Jon. *From This Earth.* San Francisco: the author, 1969.
Collection of photographs about the farm workers' strike.

Lillard, Richard. "The Soil Beneath the Blacktop," in Carey McWilliams, ed., *The California Revolution.* New York: Grossman, 1968, pp. 147-158.
California's agricultural industry: its changing character, current problems, and future prospects.

London, Joan and Henry Anderson. *So Shall Ye Reap.* New York: Crowell, 1970. 208 pp. Available in paperback, Apollo Books, 1971.
Brief historical perspective of farm labor in California from the 1880s to the present, with the last two chapters devoted to Cesar Chavez and UFWOC. Discusses agribusiness, early attempts to organize, and the activities of Ernesto Galarza, Fred Van Dyke, and Fr. Thomas McCullough.

Ludwig, Edward and James Santibanez, eds. *The Chicanos: Mexican American Voices.* Baltimore: Penguin Books, 1971. 286 pp.
Anthology of fiction and non-fiction. A number of the selections are about, or contain references to, Cesar Chavez, UFWOC, farm workers, farm labor organizing, and the farm workers theater. Contributors include Cesar Chavez, Raymond Barrio, Luis Valdez, Joan Baez, Philip Ortego, Reies Lopez Tijerina, and Enrique Lopez.

McDonald, James G. *To Eat or Not to Eat California's Grapes, That is the Question!* Toronto: Don Mills United Church, Sept. 1, 1969. 16 pp.
Opposes boycott.

McWilliams, Carey. *Factories in the Field: The Story of Migratory Farm Labor in California.* Boston: Little, Brown and Co., 1939. 334 pp. Revised edition, Hamden, Conn.: Shoe String Press, 1969.
Social history of California; exploitation of farm labor; why "farming has been replaced by industrialized agriculture, the farm by the farm factory." Discusses land monopolization and the growth of agribusiness, strikes and various attempts at unionization, foreign workers, vigilantes and riots, and growers' organizations. Bibliography is dated but useful.

McWilliams, Carey [*Continued*]

———. *Ill Fares the Land: Migrants and Migratory Labor in the United States.* Boston: Little, Brown and Co., 1942. Re-issued by Barnes and Noble, 1967. 419 pp.
Study of the "agricultural revolution." Includes information on the LaFollette Committee investigations, child labor, mechanization, labor contractors, legislation, strikes, living and working conditions, areas of the country when large numbers of migrant workers are used, the Industrial Workers of the World (IWW), Agricultural and Cannery Workers Union, National Farm Laborer's Union, Agricultural Workers' Industrial Union, Southern Tenant Farmers Union, and the Associated Farmers of California. Bibliography is dated but useful.

———. *The Mexicans in America: A Students Guide to Localized History.* New York: Teachers College Press, Columbia University, 1968. 32 pp.
Brief summary for high school students. Mentions bracero program, grape strike, Cesar Chavez, and the unionization of farm workers in California and Texas.

———. *North From Mexico: The Spanish-Speaking People of the United States.* New York: Greenwood Press, 1968. 324 pp.
Originally published in 1949 (New York: Lippincott), this edition contains a new introduction by the author. Information on braceros, migrant workers, and early attempts to unionize farm workers.

Matthiessen, Peter. *Sal Si Puedes: Cesar Chavez and the New American Revolution.* New York: Random House, 1970. 372 pp. Available in paperback, Delta Books.
Expansion of Matthiessen's two-part article, "Organizer: Profile of Cesar Chavez," in *New Yorker*, June 21 and 28, 1969. Background information on Cesar Chavez and the origins and development of the National Farm Workers Association and UFWOC.

Meier, Matt S. and Feliciano Rivera. *The Chicanos: A History of Mexican Americans.* New York: Hill and Wang, 1972. 302 pp. Available in paperback.
Includes information on UFWOC and past farm labor strikes and efforts to organize.

Metzler, William H. *Farm Mechanization and Labor Stabilization.* Research Report No. 280. Davis, Calif.: University of California, Giannini Foundation of Agricultural Economics, January, 1965. 58 pp.

———. *The Farm Worker in a Changing Agriculture.* Research Report No. 277. Davis, Calif.: University of California, Giannini Foundation of Agricultural Economics, September, 1964. 98 pp.

Moore, Joan W. *Mexican Americans.* Englewood Cliffs, N.J.: Prentice Hall, 1970. 172 pp.
Primarily an urban sociological study but contains a few references to agricultural labor, Chavez, and UFWOC.

———. *Mexican-Americans: Problems and Prospects.* Institute for Research on Poverty, University of Wisconsin. Madison: University of Wisconsin Press, 1966. 56 pp.

Moore, Truman E. *The Slaves We Rent.* New York: Random House, 1965. 171 pp.
Migrant farm workers throughout the country: living and working conditions, braceros, Migrant Ministry, agribusiness and the plight of the small farmer, past efforts to unionize farm workers, AWOC, and NFWA.

Moquin, Wayne and Charles Van Doren, eds. *A Documentary History of the Mexican Americans.* New York: Praeger, 1971. 413 pp. Available in paperback, Bantam Books, 1972. 517 pp.

Morin, Alexander. *Organizability of Farm Labor in the United States.* Harvard Studies in Labor in Agriculture, No. 2-HL. Cambridge: Harvard University Press, 1952. 102 pp.

Myers, Robin. *The Position of Farm Workers in Federal anu State Legislation.* New York: National Advisory Committee on Farm Labor, 1959.51 pp. Covers workmen's compensation, unemployment compensation, labor camps, collective bargaining, residence laws, minimum wage, labor contractors, housing, transportation, and child labor. Notes and bibliography.

National Advisory Committee on Farm Labor. *Agribusiness and Its Workers.* New York, 1963. 48 pp.
The growth of agribusiness, decline of family farms, living and working conditions, and legislation.

———. *Farm Labor Organizing, 1905-1967: A Brief History.* New York, 1967. 68 pp.

———. *The Grape Strike.* New York, February, 1966. 35 pp.
Background on AWOC, NFWA, and the origins and early events of the Delano grape strike.

———. *Poverty on the Land.* A Report on the Public Hearings Held By the National Advisory Committee on Farm Labor, Washington, D.C., May 18-19, 1964. New York, 1965, 64 pp.
P.L. 78, P.L. 414, agribusiness, federal and state legislation and public assistance, housing, health, employment conditions. Notes, findings, recommendations, and list of participants.

National Advisory Committee on Farm Labor (Continued)

———. *Report on Farm Labor.* Public Hearings of the National Advisory Committee on Farm Labor, Washington, D.C., February 5-6, 1959. 40 pp.

National Agricultural Workers Union. *The Blight on the Countryside: A Brief Illustrated Over-view of a National Problem.* Washington, D.C., 1959. 10 pp.

———. *Workers In Our Fields, 1934-1959.* 25th Anniversary Booklet. Washington, D.C., 1959. 38 pp.
Formation of the union (Southern Tenant Farmers Union); early cotton strikes; LaFollette Committee investigations; United Cannery, Agricultural, Packing and Allied Workers: DiGiorgio strike (1947); President's Commission on Migratory Labor; wetbacks; and braceros. Includes photographs, songs, and biographical sketches of STFU and NAWU officers.

Nava, Julian. *The Mexican American: An Anthology of Basic Readings (From the Beginnings to the Present).* New York: Van Nostrand Reinhold Co., 1971.

Nelkin, Dorothy. *On the Season: Aspects of the Migrant Labor System.* Ithaca: New York State School of Industrial and Labor Relations, Cornell University, 1970. 85 pp.

Nelson, Eugene. *Huelga: The First Hundred Days of the Great Delano Grape Strike.* Delano, California: Farm Worker Press, 1966. 122 pp.

North, David S. *The Border Crossers: People Who Live in Mexico and Work in the United States.* Washington: TransCentury Corp., 1970. 319 pp.
"Motivation for the study was a concern about the impact that the commuting workers have on the resident American work force in an area where wages are generally low and unemployment high."

Padfield, Harland and William E. Martin. *Farmers, Workers and Machines: Technological and Social Change in Farm Industries of Arizona,* Tucson: University of Arizona Press, 1965. 325 pp.

Parker, Carleton H. *The Casual Laborer and Other Essays.* New York: Harcourt, Brace and Howe, 1920. 199 pp. Reissued, New York: Russell and Russell, 1967.
Essays about the IWW and their activities with farm workers. Includes Parker's Report on the Wheatland Hop Fields Riot.

Pesticides: The Poisons We Eat. Delano, Calif.: United Farm Workers Organizing Committee, 1969. 16 pp.
Describes various pesticides and their effects upon farm workers and consumers.

Pitrone, Jean Maddern. *Chavez: Man of the Migrants.* New York: Alba House, 1971. 169 pp. Also published by Pyramid Books: (New York, 1972). Both are paperback.

Biographical sketch of Cesar Chavez and discussion of his efforts to organize farm workers.

Pontier, Raymond J. *Report From Delano: Observations on the Grape Dispute.* Clifton, N.J.: Christian Action Commission, Reformed Church in America, February 12, 1969. 7 pp.
Observations based upon the author's visit to the Delano area and interviews with growers and UFWOC leaders.

Proctor, Ben. "The Modern Texas Rangers: A Law-Enforcement Dilemma in the Rio Grande Valley," in Manuel P. Servin, *The Mexican-Americans: An Awakening Minority.* Beverly Hills, Calif.: Glencoe Press, 1970, pp. 212-227.
Strike at La Casita Farms, the March to Austin, NFWA, and the blocking of Roma Bridge.

The Public's Stake in the Anti-Consumer Grape Boycott. Washington, D.C.: Consumers' Rights Committee, [1969]. 33 pp.
Presents an anti-boycott point of view. Discusses background of strike and boycott, unionization, financial support, church involvement, labor laws, mechanization, "greencarders," pesticides, and nonviolence.

Rendon, Armando. *Chicano Manifesto.* New York: Macmillan, 1971. 337 pp.
Contains a number of references to Cesar Chavez and farm workers.

Romano, Octavio I., ed. *El Espejo: The Mirror.* Berkeley, Calif.: Quinto Sol Publications, 1969.
Anthology of Mexican American literature.

———. *Voices: Selected Readings From EL GRITO.* Berkeley, Calif,: Quinto Sol Publications, 1970. 211 pp.
Includes "The Mexican American and the Church," by Cesar Chavez.

Roy, Ewell Paul. *Collective Bargaining in Agriculture.* Danville, Ill,: Interstate Printers and Publishers, 1970. 280 pp.

Samora, Julian. *Los Mojados: The Wetback Story.* Notre Dame: University of Notre Dame Press, 1971.

———, ed. *La Raza: Forgotten Americans.* Notre Dame: University of Notre Dame Press, 1966. 218 pp.
Collection of essays. Includes information on the problems of migrant workers.

Schmidt, Fred H. *After the Bracero: An Inquiry Into the Problems of Farm Labor Recruitment.* Los Angeles: Institute of Industrial Relations, University of California, 1964. 139 pp. + 32 pp.
Concludes that farmers need "a more adequate and stable domestic supply," and farm laborers need a more adequate and stable income, including unemployment insurance.

Schwartz, Harry. *Seasonal Farm Labor in the United States, With Special Reference to Hired Workers in Fruit and Vegetable and Sugar-Beet Production.* Columbia University Studies in the History of American Agriculture, No. 11. New York: Columbia University Press, 1945. 172 pp.
Includes some discussion of various strikes, attempts at unionization, and child labor.

Selvin, David F. *Sky Full of Storm: A Brief History of California Labor.* Berkeley: University of California, Institute of Industrial Relations, Center For Labor Research and Education, 1966. 86 pp.
Sections on various attempts at farm labor organizing, farm strikes, braceros, AWOC, and NFWA.

Servin, Manuel P. *The Mexican-Americans: An Awakening Minority.* Beverly Hills, Calif.: Glencoe Press, 1970. 235 pp.
Anthology, including some historical studies previously unpublished. Last two chapters, dealing with the period since World War II, especially relevant. Well-documented.

Sherry, Gerard E., comp. *Farm Labor Problems: The Anguish of Delano.* In Spanish, *Problemas Del Trabajo Agricola: La Angustia de Delano.* [Fresno, Calif.: Diocese of Fresno, n.d.] 29 pp.
Compilation of material previously published in the Fresno Diocese weekly publication, *Central California Register.* Contains statement of Bishop Hugh Donahoe before the Senate Subcommittee on Migratory Labor, interview with Cesar Chavez, interview with Delano growers, editorial on church views, and statement by California bishops on the NLRA.

Shotwell, Louisa R. *The Harvesters: The Story of the Migrant People.* Garden City, N.Y.: Doubleday, 1961.
Good in national statistics regarding migrant labor; national and state legislation; background on farm unions, California Migrant Ministry, and farm labor contractors.

Simmen, Edward, ed. *The Chicano: From Caricature to Self-Portrait.* New York: Mentor, 1971. 318 pp.
Collection of short stories, 1869-1970.

———. *Pain and Promise: The Chicano Today.* New York: Mentor, 1972. 348 pp.
Collection of essays.

Steiner, Stan. *La Raza: The Mexican Americans.* New York: Harper & Row, 1970. 418 pp. Available in paperback, Harper Colophon Books.
Contains a number of references to Chavez, UFWOC, and the grape boycotts.

Sturt, Daniel W. *The Rural Manpower Center Program in 1967.* Mimeograph No. 6. Lansing: Michigan State University, Rural Manpower Center, January, 1968. 26 pp.

Taylor, Ronald B. *Sweatshops in the Sun: Child Labor on the Farm.* Boston: Beacon Press, 1973. 216 pp.

Terzian, James and Kathryn Cramer. *Mighty Hard Road: The Story of Cesar Chavez.* New York: Doubleday, 1970. 136 pp.
Children's book. Chavez, Community Service Organization, formation of NFWA, grape strike, sources of support, and merger with AWOC.

The Truth About the Grape Boycott. Chicago: American Farm Bureau Federation, April, 1969. 23 pp.
"There is no strike." "The union does not represent workers." Includes Farm Bureau's solution to farm labor problems.

United Automobile Workers, Canadian Region. *Canada's Flag Flies in California's Grapefields.* Windsor, Ontario, 1969. 39 pp.
Photographs and text depicting the visit to California of Canadian trade union, student, church, and political representatives in support of the grape strike and boycott. Includes statements by Cesar Chavez and Dennis McDermott, director of the UAW's Canadian Region.

The Use of Mexican Contract Nationals and Its Effects on the Employment of Domestic Agricultural Workers in the Imperial Valley of California. National Agricultural Workers Union, August, 1953. 33 pp.

The Uses of U.C. Berkeley: Research. Berkeley, Calif.: Radical Student Union, 1969. 56 pp.
Section on agribusiness—"how the university [of California] is used to develop machinery and techniques for the agricultural industry at no cost to the growers" — is adapted from Draper, *The Dirt on California (Berkeley: The Independent Socialist Clubs of America. 1968).*

Valdez, Luis and Stan Steiner, eds. *Aztlan: An Anthology of Mexican American Literature.* New York: Knopf, 1972.

Wagner, Nathaniel N. and Marsha J. Haug. *Chicanos: Social and Psychological Perspectives.* St. Louis: C.V. Mosby Co., 1971. 303 pp.
Collection of recent articles with chapter introductions by the authors.

Weiner, Sandra. *Small Hands, Big Hands: Seven Profiles of Chicano Migrant Workers and Their Families.* New York: Pantheon Books, 1970. 55 pp.
Children's book. Profiles based upon interviews with farm workers, both children and adults, in California.

The Wetback Strike: A Report on the Strike of Farm Workers in the Imperial Valley of California, May 24-June 25, 1951. Washington, D.C.: National Farm Labor Union, 1951. 23 pp.
"The strike was against 'wetback' labor conditions imposed upon American workers by the Imperial Valley Farmers' Association." Strike was complicated by the use of Mexican Nationals as strikebreakers and the refusal of the Labor Department to remove them from the area.

What About the Boycott of California Grapes? A Reply to the California Grape Growers. [Delano, Calif.]: United Farm Workers, October 28, 1968. 11 pp.
UFWOC replies to various statements and charges made by growers.

Which Road to Farm Labor Peace? Delano, Calif.: South Central Farmers Committee, [1969].
Presents the growers' viewpoint regarding national legislation.

Wilson, Kirke. *A Brief History of the Bracero System and Its Impact on Farm Labor in California.* Pasadena, Calif.: American Friends Service Committee, Farm Workers Opportunity Project, 1967. 20 pp.

Witney, Fred. *Agricultural Workers Under National Labor Relations Laws.* University of Illinois, Institute of Labor and Industrial Relations Bulletin, Series A, Vol. 2, special, March, 1948. 32 pp.

Wollenberg, Charles. "Conflict in the Fields: Mexican Workers in California Agri-Business," in Charles Wollenberg, ed., *Ethnic Conflict in California History.* Los Angeles: Tinnon-Brown, 1970, pp. 137-152.

Wright, Dale. *They Harvest Despair: The Migrant Farm Worker.* Boston: Beacon Press, 1965.
Study of migrant labor in the East. Author spent six months working with migrant crews.

Zermeno, Andy and *El Malcriado. Don Sotaco: Cartoons From the Delano Strike.* Delano, Calif.: Farm Worker Press, 1966.

Articles

Adair, Doug. "California Vineyards Revisited." *Catholic Worker*, 33(September, 1967), 5.

———. "Cesar Chavez's Biggest Battle." *Nation*, 205 (December 11, 1967), 627-628.
Strike against Giumarra, financial problems.

———. "A Season of Hope For Farm Workers." *Catholic Worker*, 36 (June, 1970), 3+.
Background on the table grape boycott: difficulties encountered, contracts signed with a few small growers, prospects for ending the grape strike and boycott.

———. "Texas Strike." *Liberation*, 12 (August, 1967), 6-9.
Farm workers strike in Starr County, Texas.

Adams, John P. "Churches' Migrant Ministry Brings Contact With Mexican Americans." *Engage*, 1(August 1-15, 1969), 20-21.

"AFL-CIO Organizers Go After Farm Labor." *Business Week*, September 24, 1960, pp. 50-58.
AWOC in California, earlier attempts to organize farm workers, P.L. 78 and braceros, minimum wage, housing, and mechanization.

"Again la Huelga." *Time*, 101(May 7, 1973), 79.
Grape strike in Coachella Valley.

"The Agricultural Labor Problem." *Journal of Farm Economics*, 58 (December, 1966), 1121-1153.

"Agriculture and the Worker." *American Labor*, 4 (April, 1971), 44-55.
UFWOC, current and proposed legislation for workers and growers.

Aguirre, Lydia R. "The Meaning of the Chicano Movement." *Social Casework*, 52 (May, 1971), 259-261.

"Alberta's Sugar-beet Workers." *Canadian Labour*. 16(January, 1971), 15+.

Allen, Gary. "The Grape Communist Wrath in Delano." *American Opinion*, 9(June, 1966), 1-14.
"Phony strike" supported by communists.

Allen, Steve. "Migrant Workers in Your State: Must They Work Dirt Cheap?" *Coronet*, March, 1967, pp. 150-194.

"The Ambiguity of Awards." *Christian Century*, 87 (November 4, 1970), 1308.
Cesar Chavez turns down Family of Man Award from Council of Churches of New York City (bronze medallion and $2000). Reason: "Achievements of UFWOC on behalf of social justice and nonviolence are not an individual affair. . . ."

"American Farm Labor Replaces Braceros." *Christian Century,* 84(February 1, 1967), 133; and 84 (March 8, 1967), 316.

"American Farm Workers Need Protection of Federal Labor Law," *International Teamster,* 70(January, 1973), 16-18.
Frank Fitzsimmons, Teamster General President, addresses American Farm Bureau Federation convention—summary of speech.

"America's Ongoing Agricultural Revolution." *Social Justice Review,* 63 (March, 1971), 418.

Anderson, Henry. "The Grape Strike and the Concept of Staying Power." Citizens for Farm Labor, *Farm Labor,* 4(March, 1966), 13-16.

———. "In Dubious Battle, 1965." Citizens For Farm Labor, *Farm Labor,* 3 (May, 1965), 5-7.
Termination of P.L. 78, P.L. 414; visit to Salinas Valley by Secretary of Labor Willard Wirtz.

———. "Picketing In Perspective: An Editorial." Citizens For Farm Labor, *Farm Labor,* 4(March, 1966), 5-6.
Impossible to strike against all the growers in all the various crops. Need legislation and need more interested individuals and organizations lobbying for legislation.

———. "To Build A Union." Citizens For Farm Labor, *Farm Labor,* Vol. 4, Nos. 4-6 (1966).
Three-part article originally written in 1961 when the author was director of research for AWOC. Discusses problems of unionizing agricultural workers and suggests some possible answers.

Angell, J. "The Grape Boycott." *American Society of Farm Managers and Rural Appraisers Journal,* 34(April, 1970), 67-70.

"An Appeal to Congress." *America,* 119 (September 14, 1968), 176-177.
Editorial: need to amend NLRA; farm labor legislation.

"An Appraisal on the New Labor Bill." *American Fruit Grower,* 89 (May, 1969), 8.
Farm Bureau-sponsored bill on labor relations in agriculture introduced by Senator Murphy.

"Arizona Law Curbs Farm Union." *U.S. News,* 72 (June 5, 1972), 102.
Describes provisions of the law.

"Asparagus Aspersions." *Newsweek,* 65 (April 5, 1965), 34.
Secretary of Labor Wirtz to decide if government will allow Mexican workers into country to pick asparagus and other vegetables; growers claim shortage of domestic workers.

Auerbach, Jerold S. "The LaFollette Committee: Labor and Civil Liberties in the New Deal." *Journal of American History*, 51(December, 1964), 435-459.

Awner, Max. "New Hope For Braceros." *Progressive*, 28(August, 1964), 21-24.

Baird, James W. "Farm Strike in California: Another View." *Presbyterian Life*, 19(February 1, 1966), 26-28.
"Church should be involved . . . but its place should be redemptive . . . rather than narrowly partisan."

Baker, George. "Chavez and the Teamsters: Showdown in the Coachella Valley." *Ramparts*, 12(August-September, 1973), 28-31+.

Ball, Charles E. "Farm Labor: What You Can Expect From Union Organizers." *Farm Journal*, 96(May, 1972), 32+.
Interview with Cesar Chavez.

Bank, John. "Cesar Chavez—What He Now Wants For Farm Workers," *St. Anthony Messenger*, 78(April, 1971), 16-26.
Background on Chavez, UFWOC, and early attempts to unionize farm workers. Grape strike and boycott; lettuce strike and boycott, court injunction, Chavez jail term; opposition to UFWOC; pesticides.

———. "Chavez: Third World Organizer." *Maryknoll*, 64(June, 1970), 48-53.
Cesar Chavez and UFWOC. Need of the poor to organize.

———. "Coachella Valley: Struggle For Self-Determination." *Christianity and Crisis*, 33(July 9, 1973), 132-135.
Grape contracts, UFW, Teamsters.

———. "Farm Labor Laws: Breaking UFWOC's Back." *Christianity and Crisis*. 32(March 6, 1972), 39-44.

Barker, Neil D. and Wayne C. Hartmire, Jr. "The Grape Strike." *Together*, 10(September, 1966), 42-47.

Barnes, Peter. "Reagan Versus the Poverty Lawyers." *New Republic*, 164(Jan. 23, 1971), 15-17. Reply, Leonard C. Battle, 164(February 13, 1971), 33.
California Rural Legal Assistance.

Barr, Gerald. "Cesar Chavez: Apostle of Non-Violence," *Observer*, May, 1970.
Interview with Cesar Chavez.

"Battle of the Grapes." *Reader's Digest*, 95(October, 1969), 88-92.
Abridgement of "The Little Strike That Grew to La Causa," *Time*, July 4, 1969.

"Battle Over the Braceros." *Business Week*, January 9, 1965, p. 24.

Bauer, Charles. "Plight of California Grape-Pickers." *Canadian Labour*, 14(November, 1969), 34.

Bauman, Albert. "Organizing Farm Labor." *St. Joseph's Magazine*, 67(March, 1966), 2.
Editorial.

Becket, James W. "A Career Ladder For Farmworkers." *Farm Labor Developments*, December, 1969, pp. 7-11.
Discusses retraining of workers who will be replaced as farming becomes more mechanized.

Beecher, John. "To the Rear, March! 1965-1940 . . ." in Bracero Politics: A Special Report." *Ramparts*, 4(September, 1965). 14-32.

Bell, Joseph N. "Harvest of Hunger." *Good Housekeeping*, 175(September, 1972), 106-107+.

"A Bell For Delano." *UAW Solidarity*, 13(May, 1970), 16.

Bennett, Fay. "Still the Harvest of Shame." *Commonweal*, 80(April 10, 1964), 83-86.
General background on farm labor, P.L. 78, pesticides, legislation, wages, and living and working conditions.

Bergman, G.M. "Self-help For the Single Farm Worker." *Christian Century*. 86(November 5, 1969), 1426+.
Lack of off-season unemployment compensation or welfare forces workers to go to skid rows. California subsidizes agribusiness in the development of new machinery but does not subsidize farm workers.

Berman, Jerry J. and Jim Hightower. "Chavez and the Teamsters." *Nation*, 211(November 2, 1970), 427-431.
Lettuce, Salinas Valley.

Bernstein, Harry. "Duel in the Sun: Union Busting, Teamster Style." *Progressive*, 37(July, 1973), 17-20.

"Beyond Peace At Delano," *America*, 123(August 22, 1970), 80.
Newsnote: Although grape strike is settled, there still are many unorganized farm workers throughout the country. Need for legislation.

"Bishops Support Cesar Chavez." *America*, 122(May 30, 1970), 574.
Editorial comment: Bishop Donnelly and Msgr. Higgins support Chavez against charges of communism.

"Bitter Grapes." *Supermarketing*, 25(June, 1970), 14-15.
Takes a middle position regarding grape boycott; considers the supermarkets to be the real victims.

"Bitter Harvest." *Free Labour World*, No.233 (November, 1969), 5-9.
Grape strike; background on Chavez, NFWA, AWOC, UFWOC, pesticides, boycotts, legislation.

Black, Roe C. "Why Not a Judicial Solution to Farm Labor Disputes?" *Top Op*[erator], 3(June, 1971), 46.

Editorial: recommends an Agricultural Labor Relations Board.

"The Black Eagle Wins." *Time*, 96 (August 10, 1970), 10-11.

UFWOC contract with Giumarra and 25 other major grape growers.

"Black(Lists) and White." *New Republic*, 159(October 26, 1968), 7-8.

Various boycotts of brand names and products, including grapes.

"Blue-Sky Sweatshop." *American Federationist*, 71(June, 1964),7-12.

Farm labor in the U.S.

Bongartz, Roy. "La Raza In Revolt." *Nation*, 210(July 1, 1970), 664-666.

Booth, P. "Sickness Insurance and California Farm Workers." *Social Security Bulletin*, 31(May, 1968), 3-13.

Borin, Elliot K. "Migrants." *Canner/Packer*, 138(February, 1969), 17-23.

Boutilier, Eugene. "The Grape Strike Today." *Engage*, 1(October 1, 1968), 10+.

Table grape strike and boycott, need for legislation.

———. "Legislation: An Answer." *Concern*, 9(August 1-15, 1967), 10-13+.

Need for labor legislation for farm workers.

———. "The New Crop of Farm Labor Legislation." *Engage*, 2(November 15, 1969), 15.

Grower proposals and UFWOC proposals.

"The Boycott Against Fresh Table Grapes." *American Fruit Grower*, 88(September, 1968), 7-8.

"Boycott of California Grapes Spreads." *Canadian Labour*, 13 (December, 1968), 38.

"Boycott Report." *New Yorker*, 48(September 2, 1972), 20-21.

Jose Gomez and New York lettuce boycott; interview with Cesar Chavez in New York.

"Bracero Politics: A Special Report." *Ramparts*, 4(September, 1965), 14-32.

William Turner: "No Dice For Braceros"

John Beecher: "To the Rear, March! 1965-1940. . ."

"Breakthrough Agreement in Coachella Valley." *Christian Century*, 87(April 22, 1970), 469.

Newsnote: signing of first contracts between UFWOC and table grape growers.

"Breakthrough For La Huelga." *Time*, 93(June 27, 1969), 18.

Ten table-grape growers announce they will negotiate with UFWOC.

"Breakthrough in Grape Strike." *Catering Industry Employee*, 79(August, 1970), 8.

Bree, John L. "An Open Letter to Jack Pickett." *California Farmer*, 230 (January 18, 1969), 8C

Author is member of California Grape Products Corp., Delano. Problems of Delano growers are those of *all* farmers; should rely on themselves and not on the government.

"Bring Back the Braceros." *Newsweek*, 65(March 8, 1965), 78.

Not enough domestic workers to fill the void left by the expiration of P.L. 78; need to bring in more Mexican laborers under Immigration Act (P.L. 414).

Brockway, Allan R. "Huelga." *Concern*, 9(August 1-15, 1967), 4-9+.

Strike in Rio Grande Valley/Starr County, Texas.

———. "Outside the Melting Pot." *Engage*, 1(August 1-15, 1969), 4-10+.

Mexican Americans, Tony Orendain, Reynaldo de la Cruz.

Brohm, Theodore L. "Grape Strike Is Termed Political, Economic Issue." *Lutheran Witness Reporter*, October 6, 1968.

Brown, Robert McA. "Cesar Chavez." *The Lamp*, January, 1971, p.21.

Brief sketch of Chavez: his personality and principles of non violence.

———. "Farm Strike In California: Should the Church Take Sides?" *Presbyterian Life*, 18(December 1,1965), 24-26.

Church should support striking farm laborers.

———. "Macedonian Plea From California." *Christianity and Crisis*. 25(November 15, 1965), 238.

California Migrant Ministry, Wayne Hartmire, Cesar Chavez, farm workers' strike.

"Brown Power." *Newsweek*, 71(March 25, 1968), 37.

Brown power movement among the Southwest's Mexican Americans; Reies Lopez Tijerina, Cesar Chavez.

Bryant, Arthur C. "Hunger and Servitude." *Metanoia*, 2(March, 1970), 1-4.

Wages and living and working conditions of farm workers in New York; grape strike and boycott; need for collective bargaining legislation.

Buckley, William F., Jr. "The Chavez Machine." *National Review*, 23(August 10, 1971), 888-889.

Efforts of UFWOC to defeat California Senate Bill 40.

———. "Don't Eat Grapes Along With Me." *National Review*, 21(July 15, 1969), 715.

———. "Victory of Cesar Chavez." *National Review*, 22(September 8, 1970), 965.

"California Bishops and the NLRA." *America,* 118(June 15, 1968), 764.

"California Bishops Speak." *Ave Maria,* 103(April 30, 1966), 4-5.

"The California Farm Workers and the Grape Boycott." *Migration Today,* 13(Autumn, 1969), 48+.

California Farmer, 224(March 19, 1966).
Almost entire issue (about 20 articles) is devoted to Cesar Chavez, UFWOC, the grape strike, and related subjects.

"California Grape Boycott." *Trans-Action,* 6(February, 1969), 6-7.
Newsnote: background of strike and boycott.

"California Grape Dispute: International Support Still Needed." *New Dawn,* Journal of the Union of Shop, Distributive and Allied Workers, 24(August, 1970), 437-438.

"California Has Yet to Get a Vacation From Labor Headlines: Early Reports Indicate She No Longer Is Alone." *American Fruit Grower,* 88(May, 1968), 8.
Organizing farm workers in California, Ohio, Michigan, and New York.

"Campaign to Boycott Lettuce." *U.S. News,* 73(August 28, 1972), 51.

"Can Farm Workers Organize?" *Current,* No. 53(November, 1964), 41-43.

"Can They Pull Off a Nationwide Boycott?" *Nation's Business,* 56(October, 1968), 46-48.
UFWOC grape boycott is a means of coercing workers into joining a union they do not want to join.

"Canadian Boycott Key Factor in UFWOC Victory." *Canadian Labour,* 15(October, 1970), 14.

"The Candor That Refreshes." *Time,* 96(August 10, 1970), 59.
Treatment of migrant workers in Florida by Coca Cola. Attempts made to remedy conditions.

Cannon, Grant. "Farm Labor Organizes: The AFL-CIO Makes Its Bid For Farm Labor in California." *Farm Quarterly,* 16(Spring, 1961), 60-65+.
Extensive description of Agricultural Workers Organizing Committee: its structure and organization, leaders, goals, and activities.

Carrera, Anna F. "The Effects of the Federal Minimum Wage on Hired Farmworkers." *Farm Labor Developments,* May, 1968, pp. 12-19.

Cauchois, Scott, Jr. and Theodore P. Lianos. "Some Economic Effects of Farm Labor Unionization." *University of Akron Business Review,* 1(Summer, 1970), 45-55.

"Cesar Chavez." *Canner/Packer,* 136(March, 1967), 28-31, cover.
Interview with Chavez.

"Cesar Chavez." *Extension,* 61(June, 1966), 15.

"Cesar Chavez: 'La Causa' and the Man." *American Labor,* 4(February, 1971), cover, 20-30.
Profile of Cesar Chavez and UFWOC.

"Cesar Losing Salad Touch." *Western Grower and Shipper,* April, 1971.

"Cesar's War." *Time,* 91(March 22, 1968), 23.
Brief background information on Cesar Chavez, the grape strike and boycott, NFWA, and Chavez's 25-day fast.

Chandler, Russell. "Trampling Out the Vintage: Squeeze on California Table Grapes." *Christianity Today,* 12(September 13, 1968), 52.
Table grape boycott, church support and opposition.

Chase, Jonathan B. "The Migrant Farm Worker in .Colorado—The Life and the Law." *University of Colorado Law Review,* 40(Fall, 1967), 45-78.

Chavez, Cesar. "Creative Nonviolence." *Catholic Worker,* June, 1969.

———. "Letter From Delano." *Christian Century,* 86(April 23, 1969), 539-540.
Open letter to growers: nonviolence, goals.

———. "The Mexican-American and the Church." *El Grito,* 1(Summer, 1968), 9-12.

———. "Nonviolence Still Works." *Look,* 33(April 1, 1969), 52-57.
Interview with Cesar Chavez.

———. "The Organizer's Tale" in "Huelga! Tales of the Revolution." *Ramparts,* 5(July, 1966), 43-50.

———. "Peregrinacion, Penitencia, Revolucion." *Town and Country Church,* 188(May-June, 1966), 16.

———. "Sharing the Wealth," in "Bring Us Together," *Playboy,* 17 (January, 1970), 127+.
"Bring Us Together" also contains articles by Senator George McGovern, Julian Bond, and Tom Wicker.

———. "We Are Not Agricultural Implements, We Are Men." *Canadian Labour,* 14(June, 1969), 32.

———. "Working Together For the Poor and For Peace." *Metanoia,* 2 (March, 1970), 5-7+.

"Chavez, Cesar (Estrada)." *Current Biography,* 30 (February, 1969), 8-11.

"Chavez Blight Spreads East." *Nation's Business,* 60 (May, 1972), 32-35.
UFWOC organizing farm workers in Florida.

"Chavez Is Jailed For Refusing to Call Off the Lettuce Boycott." *Advance,* 56 (December 26, 1970), 2.

"Chavez: One Battle Ends, Another Begins." *U.S. News*, 69 (August 10, 1970), 49-51.
End of grape strike and boycott; beginning of fruit and vegetable strike in Salinas Valley; Teamsters.

"Chavez Pickets Again." *Christian Century*, 90 (January 17, 1973), 64.
Newsnote: California Supreme Court decision lifting injunction against UFW's striking and picketing.

"Chavez Strikes Again." *Newsweek*, 77 (January 25, 1971), 64+.
Suit against the Defense Department. Lettuce strike and boycott; Teamsters.

"Cheer Grape Strikers: UAW's 'Most Solemn Pledge'." *UAW Solidarity*, 9(June, 1966), 11.
UAW convention delegates pledge to support UFWOC strike.

"Chicanos Campaign For a Better Deal." *Business Week*, May 29, 1971, pp. 48-53.
Special report on the increasing activism of Mexican Americans. Discusses various organizations and leaders including Cesar Chavez and UFWOC, Reies Lopez Tijerina and the Alianza Federal de Pueblos Libres, Corky Gonzales and the Crusade For Justice, and La Raza Unida.

"Child Labor, 1968." *International*, September, 1968, pp. 18-22.

"Child Labor, 1971." *Newsweek*, 77(April 12, 1971), 83-84.
Child labor in agriculture.

"Churches Oppose Bracero Program." *Christian Century*, 81(December 23, 1964), 1580-1581.
Opposition to P.L. 78 and P.L. 414.

"Churchmen and Table Grapes." *America*, 120(January 4, 1969), 4.
Editorial comment: churchmen supporting UFWOC.

"Citrus Harvest Mechanization Research." *Farm Labor Developments*, October, 1969, pp. 17-21.

Clark, Henry B. "Oppressed Farm Labor." *Christianity and Crisis*, 25(June 28, 1965), 134-135.

Cleath, Robert L. "Rendering Unto Cesar." *Christianity Today*. 14(July 3, 1970), 32-33.
Churchmen who are supporting and opposing Chavez.

Coffey, Joseph D. "National Labor Relations Legislation: Possible Impact on American Agriculture." *American Journal of Agricultural Economics*, 51(December, 1969), 1065-1074.
Discusses "costs and benefits within the agricultural sector of extending NLRA coverage to farm workers and their employers."

Cohen, Eli E. "Child Labor: A Barbarism We Must Not Tolerate." *Parents,* 46 [August, 1971], 34.

Cohen, Irving J. "Huelga! A Milestone in Farm Unionism." *Farm Labor Developments,* September, 1966, pp. 9-17.
Background information, National Labor Relations Act, AWOC, NFWA, past efforts to organize farm workers, Pilgrimage to Sacramento, DiGiorgio. Schenley, Senate hearings.

———. "La Huelga! Delano and After." *Monthly Labor Review,* 91(June, 1968), 13-16.

———. "La Huelga in Starr County, Texas." *Farm Labor Developments,* December, 1967, pp. 9-16.
"This strike has already had a profound impact on unionization of both agricultural and nonagricultural workers in the border areas."

"Coke's Migrants Get A New Deal." *Business Week,* November 14, 1970, pp. 109-110.

"Collective Bargaining on the Farm." *Monthly Labor Review,* 90(June, 1967), III-IV.
DiGiorgio contract, 1967.

"A Company That Helps Migrants." *Business Week,* March 6, 1971, p. 61.
Coca Cola in Florida.

Compton, Neville. "This Green Valley Isn't So Jolly." *New Republic,* 159(September 7, 1968), 19-20.
Migrant labor in the Yakima Valley, Washington; Tomas Villanueva and the United Farmworkers Cooperative; conditions in labor camps.

"Congress Extends Bracero Program." *Christian Century,* 81(January 1, 1964), 5.

Conrad, Ronald. "Nosotros Venceremos: Ohio Migrants Seek Power." *Here and Now,* 5(September, 1968), 1-6.
Farm Labor Organizing Committee.

"A Continuing Conversation with Cesar Chavez." *Journal of Current Social Issues,* 9(Spring, 1971), cover, 30-32.
Interview with Chavez following his speech at Riverside Church, New York City. Discusses background of farm workers' movement, Dow Chemical, Teamsters, financial support, farm labor contractors, and automation.

"Contracts in the Coachella." *Time,* 95(April 13, 1970), 21.
Signing of first contracts with Coachella table grape growers.

Conway, James F. "Migrants' Directions." *Catholic World,* 205(April, 1967), 31-35.

Conway, James F. (Continued)

———. "Migrants in the Promised Land." *America*, 115(September 10, 1966), 253-255.
Migrant workers in Utah.

Cook, Jack. "Rangers Riot, Strikers Suffer." *Catholic Worker*, 33(June, 1967), 1+.
UFWOC in Texas.

Coombs, S.W. "Bracero's Journey: U.S. Harvest Provides Seasonal Work For Mexican Farmers." *Americas*, 15(December, 1963), 7-11.
Brief history of the bracero program.

Cordtz, Dan. "Corporate Farming: A Tough Row to Hoe." *Fortune*, 86(August, 1972), 134-139+.

Corey, Fred P. "Avoiding a Collision Course With Labor Unions." *American Fruit Grower*, 90(January, 1970), 10.

Corker, Jeanne L. "Our Brother the Migrant." *Christian Century*, 82(September 29, 1965), 1192-1193.
Need for better housing for migrant workers.

"Council of Growers' Statement on Delano." *California Farmer*, 224(January 15, 1966), 11.

"Coverage Sought Under NLRB For Farm Field Workers." *IUD Agenda*, 4(January/February, 1968), 31.
Short news item.

Coyne, J.R., Jr. "Doctored Grapes?" *National Review*, 22(January 27, 1970), 88.

———. "Grapes of Wrath." *National Review*, 21(July, 1, 1969), 639.

"A Crate of Sour Grapes." *Butcher Workman*, 54(June, 1968), 16.
Editorial.

Cray, Ed. "Social Reform Through Law." *Nation*, 207(October 14, 1968), 368-372.
California Rural Legal Assistance fights illegal use of braceros to replace domestic farm workers.

Creagan, James F. "Public Law 78: A Tangle of Domestic and International Relations." *Journal of Inter-American Studies*, 7(October, 1965), 541-556.

"Crippling Farm Workers." *New Republic*, 167(September 16, 1972), 10.
Grower-sponsored legislation in a number of states, including Proposition 22 in California.

" 'Crystal Balling': The Prospects for Fruit and Vegetable Mechanization." *Farm Labor Developments*, March, 1969, pp. 16-22.

Curlee, Don. "Shattering Table Grape Experience in 1965-66." *Western Fruit Grower,* January, 1966, pp. 19-22.
About the growers and their merchandizing problems: "sad marketing experience." No mention of strike or NFWA.

Currier, Betty. "The Farm Workers' Story . . . Another Side to the Farm Labor Strife." *California Farm Bureau Monthly,* December, 1968.

Davis, Thurston N. "Viva la Huelga!" *America,* 114(April 23, 1966), 589-590.
March from Delano to Sacramento; "Plan of Delano."

Daws, Gavan. "The Farm Worker: After 20 Years of Unions." *Farm Quarterly,* 25(Spring Planning, 1970), 58+.
History of the unionization of agricultural workers in Hawaii. Hawaii Employment Relations Act of 1945 granted the right to organize to agricultural workers not covered by the NLRA. Part of a three-article series, "The Farm Worker." The other two articles were written by William Kircher and Allan Grant.

Day, Dorothy, "On Pilgrimage." *Catholic Worker,* 35(June, 1969), 1†.
Describes visit to UFWOC headquarters (Forty Acres) in Delano and to Coachella Valley.

———. "Strike Leader." *Catholic Worker,* 35(January, 1969), 1+.
Dolores Huerta.

Day, Mark. "Bagdasarian Number Two." *Catholic Worker,* 35(July-August, 1969), 5.
Eviction of strikers from farm labor camp; beginning of UFWOC strike in Coachella Valley.

———. "The Black Eagle and Desert Grapes." *Way,* 25(September, 1969), 24-35.
Grape strike in Coachella Valley.

———. "The Clergy and the Grape Strike." *America,* 121(August 30, 1969), 114-117.
Not enough participation by clergymen, especially those in Delano.

———. "Delano: A Steak Dinner or a Plate of Beans?" *Catholic Worker,* 34(March-April, 1969), 1+.

———. "The Grape Boycott: Where Is It Now?" *National Catholic Reporter,* 6(April 24, 1970), 1+.

———. "The Grape Boycott Should Be Supported." *U.S. Catholic and Jubilee,* 35(March, 1970), 14-15+.

———. Review of London and Anderson, *So Shall Ye Reap. America,* 124(April 17, 1971), 416-418.

Day, Terence L. "A New Light on Farm Labor Problems." *Farm Quarterly,* 26(March-April, 1971), 40.
Strike at hop ranches in Washington. Court decision regarding rights of growers and of UFWOC organizers and pickets.

"Day By Day With the FWA." Citizens For Farm Labor, *Farm Labor,* 4(April, 1966), 18-24.
Chronicle of NFWA activities excerpted from California newspapers, March 17-April 23, 1966.

"Deathtrap for Wetbacks." *Time,* 92(October 11, 1968), 24-25.

Deedy, John. "The Grape Strike." *Commonweal,* 92(April 24, 1970), 130.
Newsnote.

Degnan, James P. "Monopoly In the Vineyards: The Grapes of Wrath Strike." *Nation,* 202 (February 7, 1966), 151-154.
Cesar Chavez, NFWA, AWOC, National Labor Relations Act, braceros, small growers vs. agribusiness.

"Delano: Another Selma?" *Ave Maria,* 103 (January 1, 1966), 16-17.

"Delano: Grapes of Wrath," *St. Joseph Magazine,* 67 (June, 1966), 6-22.

"Delano—A New Harvest For Migrants," *IUD Agenda,* 3(February, 1967), 19-22.
Merger of NFWA and AWOC, DiGiorgio election, Schenley agreement, and National Farm Workers Service Center (health clinic, Farm Workers Cooperative, credit union, El Teatro Campesino).

"Delano Grower Comments on Strike," *California Farmer,* 224 (January 15, 1966), 21.
Statement by Martin Zaninovich, December 23, 1965: strike composed mostly of professional pickets paid by the union. Workers do not want a union.

Dellon. Howard N. "The Adverse-Effect Policy for Agricultural Labor," *Farm Labor Developments.* August, 1966, pp. 15-26.
P.L. 78, P.L. 414: importation of foreign workers.

———. "Foreign Agricultural Workers and the Prevention of Adverse Effect." *Labor Law Journal.* 17 (December, 1966), 739-748.
". . . the use of foreign workers in seasonal agricultural activities should not be at the expense of United States citizens." P.L. 78, P.L. 414: background and discussion.

"Democrats Invade the Lettuce Patch." *Business Week,* July 22, 1972, pp. 17-18.
Lettuce boycott supported at Democratic Convention.

"Despite Its Degree of Success or Failure, the Fresh Table Grape Boycott Has Made an Impact on Agriculture." *American Fruit Grower,* 88 (November, 1968), 12-13.

DeSutter, Kathleen. "Farmworkers Versus the Pentagon." *Catholic Worker,* 37 (February, 1971), 3.

———. "Lettuce Boycott." *Catholic Worker,* 36 (October-November, 1970), 6.

"Developments In Industrial Relations." *Monthly Labor Review,* 90 (June, 1967), 72-79.
Section on UFWOC/DiGiorgio contract.

Dietzen, John. "Bishops in the Grape Strike." *Catholic Post,* August 16, 1970.
Five bishops representing the National Conference of Catholic Bishops mediate in the California grape strike.

DiGiorgio, Robert. "Statement of DiGiorgio Corporation to *Ave Maria.*" *Ave Maria,* 104 (July 2, 1966), 13+.

"DiGiorgio Drivers, Shed Workers Go Teamster in Farm Vote." *International Teamster,* 63(October, 1966), 16.
Omits mention of field workers, who voted for UFWOC.

"Dispute In Delano." *Commonweal,* 84(January 28, 1966), 491.

"Dollar Harvest: An Expose of the Farm Bureau." *American Federationist,* 76
Review of Berger's *Dollar Harvest.* (February, 1972), 21-22.

Donahue, Kathy. "Viva La Huelga!" *Textile Labor,* 39(April, 1968), 8-9.
Background on Chavez, grape strike, and grape boycott; urges textile workers to support the boycott.

Donohoe, Hugh. "Collective Bargaining for Farm Workers." *Catholic Mind,* 68(January, 1970), 24-27.

"Don't Buy Grapes," *United Teacher,* February 7, 1968, p. 8.
Giumarra grape strike.

Dorsey, Barbara. "Cesar Chavez." *National Catholic Reporter,* 4(February 14, 1968), 4.

"Dow On the Farm." *New Republic,* 163(December 12, 1970), 8.
Court injunction by Bud Antle, Inc. against UFWOC picketing; Dow Chemical's relationship to Antle.

Dowling, James G. "Delano Views: An Open Letter to *Ave Maria* Magazine." *Ave Maria,* 103(January 29, 1966), 16.

Drake, James. "Farm Workers." *Catholic Worker,* 36 (October-November, 1970), 1+.

UFWOC: origins, goals, credit union, labor contractors, Linnell-Woodville rent strike, sources of support.

Drake, Jim and Glen Gersmehl. "Salad Days At the Pentagon." *Commonweal,* 93(February 19, 1971), 485-486.

Duberman, Martin. "Grapes of Wrath." *New Republic,* 157(December 2, 1967), 23-26. Reply by William L. Kircher, *New Republic,* 158(January 6, 1968), 46-47.
Review of John Dunne's *Delano.*

duFresne, Elizabeth J. and John J. McDonnell. "The Migrant Labor Camps: Enclaves of Isolation in Our Midst." *Fordham Law Review,* 40(December, 1971), 279-304.

Dunne, John Gregory. "Strike!" *Saturday Evening Post,* 240 (May 6, 1967), 32-68.
Condensation of Dunne's *Delano.*

———. "To Die Standing: Cesar Chavez and the Chicanos." *Atlantic,* 227 (June, 1971), 39-45. Reply, J. Angell, 228 (September, 1971), 36.
Condensation of new chapter for revised edition of *Delano:* signing of grape contracts, lettuce strike, legislation, and prospects for the future.

Dyson, Lowell K. "Radical Farm Organizations and Periodicals in America, 1920-1960." *Agricultural History,* 45 (April, 1971), 111-120.

"Economic Characteristics of Migratory Workers' Families." *Farm Labor Developments,* October, 1968, pp. 20-25.
"One-fourth of all migratory workers were members of families with cash incomes of less than $2000 in 1965."

"Education of Willard Wirtz." *Nation,* 200 (April 12, 1965), 379.
Pressures on Wirtz to admit Mexican workers under regular immigration law (P.L. 414).

"Effects of Ending Bracero Program." *America,* 116 (April 15, 1967), 546.

Eisenberg, Jack. "To Be a Farm Worker." *American Federationist,* 77 (July, 1970), 12-17.
Photographs.

"El Estado de las Uvas," *Con Safos,* Vol. 2, No. 5 (1970), 3.

"*El Teatro Campesino*—Right Off the Picket Lines," *IUD Agenda,* 3 (February, 1967), 16-17.
The Farm Workers Theater: photographic essay.

"End of Bracero Program." *America,* 108 (June 22, 1963), 878-879.
House of Representatives defeats measure to extend bracero program under P.L. 78.

"The End of Public Law 78." *Farm Labor Developments,* January, 1965, pp. 1-9.

"End Run on Braceros . . . Into the 20th Century." *America,* 111 (December 19, 1964), 791.
Department of Labor hearings on substituting provisions of the Immigration and Nationality Act for the expired P.L. 78.

Engage. Vol. 1, No. 21 (August 1-15, 1969).
Contains several articles, mostly about farm workers in the Rio Grande Valley, Texas.

Erenburg, Mark. "Obreros Unidos In Wisconsin." *Monthly Labor Review,* 91(June, 1968), 17-23.
Unionization of migrant farm workers.

Ericson, Anna-Stina. "The Impact of Commuters on the Mexican-American Border Area." *Monthly Labor Review,* 93(August, 1970), 18-27.

Ernst, Jerome B. "Cesar Chavez Speaks About DiGiorgio Corporation." *Ave Maria,* 104(July 2, 1966), 12-15.

———. "Farm Labor Strikes Spread." *Extension,* 61(December, 1966), 22-25.
" . . . spreading to Wisconsin, Texas, Upstate New York, Michigan, Oregon." Strike in Texas, boycott of Delano products, Jesus Salas in Wisconsin, support from churches, mechanization, and legislation.

———. "Vagabonds . . . With a Purpose." *Extension,* 59(December, 1964), 38-40.
Volunteers working with migrants in Texas. Child labor, need for legislation.

———. "Worthy Of His Hire." *Extension,* 61(June, 1966), 11-16.
Cesar Chavez, NFWA, AWOC, Delano grape strike, California Migrant Ministry, Pilgrimage to Sacramento, need for legislation, Senate hearings. Article includes excerpt from interview with Chavez.

"European Farm Unions Support UFWOC Boycott." *Canadian Labour.* 14(April, 1969), 55.

Evans, J. Claude. "Discord Along the Rio Grande." *Christian Century,* 86(March 26, 1969), 397-400.
Editorial: Texas Council of Churches, UFWOC, Reverend Ed Krueger, Reynaldo de la Cruz.

"An Expression of Love," *Butcher Workman,* 54(July-August, 1968), 10-11.
Amalgamated Meat Cutters and Butcher Workmen make contribution to UFWOC.

Eyster, Frederick D. "My Decision to Go With the Farm Workers Ministry." *Journal of Current Social Issues.* 10(Autumn, 1972), 28-29.

"Facts About Seasonal Farm Workers in the U.S.A." *Migration Today,* 12(Spring, 1969), 23-30.
Statistical data and a brief description of UFWOC and the grape boycott.

Fallows, Marjorie. "The Mexican-American Laborers: A Different Drummer?" *Massachusetts Review,* 8(Winter, 1967), 166-176.

"Farm Labor: New Phase," *Nation,* 216(January 29, 1973), 133.
Discusses alliance between Teamsters and American Farm Bureau Federation.

"Farm Labor Breakthrough." *Progressive,* 30(August, 1966), 7-8.
Schenley contract.

"Farm Labor Drive Fizzles." *Farm Journal* (Western edition), 85(August, 1961), 10+.
AWOC.

"Farm Labor Fights an Anti-Chavez Law." *Business Week,* August 19, 1972, p. 21.
Arizona.

"Farm Labor Has No Geographical Limits." *American Fruit Grower,* 88(June, 1968), 8.
"Short labor supplies and higher wage rates face California growers . . . ."

"Farm Labor Is a Big Issue in D.C." *American Fruit Grower,* 89(June, 1969), 11.
Legislation.

"Farm Labor Legislation: Status and Prospects (as of May 26, 1965)." Citizens For Farm Labor, *Farm Labor,* 3(May, 1965), insert.

"Farm-Labor Relations in Michigan." *Farm Labor Developments,* September, 1968, pp. 10-17.

"Farm Labour Agreement Signed in California." *Labour Gazette,* 67(September, 1967), 564.

"Farm Manpower: Some Observations on 1965." *Monthly Labor Review,* 89(February, 1966), III-IV.

"Farm Union Reaps First California Victory." *Business Week,* April 16, 1966, pp. 158-160.
Schenley agrees to recognize NFWA as sole bargaining agent. Background on Chavez, NFWA, AWOC, and the Independent Farm Workers Union.

"Farm Union Turns to Community Work." *As Is,* 2(November 10, 1967), 3+.
UFWOC in California and Texas.

"Farm Vote." *Newsweek,* 68(September 12, 1966), 83-84.
DiGiorgio election: NFWA wins election against Teamsters.

"Farm Wages: Impact of the Termination of Public Law 78." *Farm Labor Developments*. October, 1965, pp. 23-25.
Termination has caused wages to go up.

"The Farm Worker." *Farm Quarterly*, 25(Spring Planning, 1970), 56-58+.
Series of three articles by William Kircher, Allan Grant, and Gavan Daws.

"The Farm Worker." *International Teamster*, 70(March, 1973), cover, 5-11.
Special report, including testimonial statements from farm workers, describing the advantages of a Teamster contract.

"The Farm Worker: His Need For Legislation." *Maine Law Review*, 22(1970), 213.

"The Farm Worker, the Small Grower, Agribusiness and the Consumer." *Monday Morning*, 34(December 15, 1969).
Report of the Council on Church and Society.

"Farm Workers." *Monthly Labor Review*, 93(October, 1970), 54-55.
No-raiding agreement with the Teamsters. Strike against Salinas area fruit and vegetable growers.

"Farm Workers." *Monthly Labor Review*, 93(November, 1970), 63.
Signing of contract with Inter Harvest, Inc., August 30, 1970.

"Farm Workers." *Union Democracy In Action*, No. 6(May, 1962), 1-6.

"Farm Workers: Target in Union Drive." *U.S. News*, 60(June 13, 1966), 124.
Independent Workers Association (of Rio Grande Valley, Texas), NFWA, AWOC, and Teamsters.

"Farm Workers—The Union Makes Them Strong." *International*, 1(February, 1968), 2-5.
New York grape boycott; Dolores Huerta; background information on the boycott and UFWOC.

"The Farm Workers Arise." *The Texas Observer*, Special Reprint, June-September, 1966, 24 pp.
Special reprint of articles in the *Texas Observer* on coverage of Texas farm workers strike. Original articles appeared in the *Observer*, June-September, 1966.

"Farm Workers Battling For a Better Life." *Seafarers Log*, 32(September, 1970), 20.

"Farm Workers Choose a Union . . . and Now the Southwest." *America*, 115(September 17, 1966), 270.
DiGiorgio election . . . farm workers' march to Austin, Texas.

"Farm Workers Fight Company Union." *Laborer*, 23(April, 1969), 13.
Agricultural Workers Freedom to Work Association.

"Farm Workers' Leader Urges Continuation of Grape Boycott Following Big Breakthrough." *Advance,* 56(June, 1970), 15.
Andy Imutan, UFWOC vice-president, speaks to Amalgamated Clothing Workers Association convention.

"Farm Workers Plead For Support of Grape Boycott." *Butcher Workman,* 54(May, 1968), 4-5.

"Farm Workers Rally in Capital." *The NMU Pilot,* 35(June, 1970), 15-16.
March and rally in Washington supported by National Maritime Union members: UFWOC members in New York accept gift of Liberty Bell replica; signing of contracts with table grape growers.

"Farm Workers Sign Landmark Contract With Grape Growers." *Catering Industry Employee,* 79(May, 1970), 7.

"Farmers Have Come Full Circle on Labor Legislation." *Farm Journal,* 96(May, 1972), 19.
News note: farmers now urging inclusion of farm workers under NLRA; Agricultural Labor Relations Act introduced in Congress.

"Farmworkers, UAW and Victory." *UAW Solidarity,* 13(July, 1970), 2.
UAW donates van to carry farmworkers' bell.

Fass, Roberta L. and Jacqueline F. Lander. "Huelga: Farm Workers Battle For Justice."*American Teacher,* 54(March, 1970), 11-14. Reprinted in United Federation of Teachers, UFT Curriculum Series, 13 pp.
Teaching unit for elementary schools: background information and lesson outlines.

"The Fate of P.L. 78." *Commonweal,* 78(June 14, 1963), 316-317.
House of Representatives refuses extension.

"Federal Legislative Status Report." *Canner/Packer,* 140(November, 1971), 16-17.
Legislation relating to agriculture and food products.

"The Fight to Organize Your Help." *Farm Journal* (Western edition), 85(February, 1961), 3+.
AWOC.

Fineberg, Richard A. "Struggle In the Vineyards." *Progressive,* 33(May, 1969), 28-31.
UFWOC, table grape boycott, agribusiness.

Fisher, Robert W. "Labor and the Economy in 1970." *Monthly Labor Review,* 94(January, 1971), 3-13.
Section on "Prolonged Stoppages" includes number of paragraphs on UFWOC strike.

Fishlow, David. "Agent Lee Is After The Subversives." *Texas Observer*, 62(August 21, 1970), 5-6.

Fitch, Bob. "Chavez: Let Us Pick Lettuce." *National Catholic Reporter*, 6(September 25, 1970), 1+.

———. "Tilting With the System." *Christian Century*. 87(February 18, 1970), 204-207.
Interview with Cesar Chavez: grape strike and boycott, labor legislation, Community Service Organization, unionization of farm workers, Migrant Ministry, and nonviolence.

Fitzsimmons, Frank E. "Teamsters and Farm Workers." *International Teamster*, 68(January, 1971), 4.
Editorial. "We still stand by our agreement with the UFWOC on jurisdiction which defines 'field labor' as belonging to the UFWOC. . . "

"For a Vote In the Vineyards." *America*, 121(November 22, 1969), 482.
News item. Critical of Catholic groups and clergy which oppose Chavez and UFWOC.

"Forbidden Fruit?: The Boycott on Grapes Is Ripe For Exposure." *Barron's*, June 2, 1969, pp. 1+.

"Foresee Long Farm Labor Conflict." *Canner/Packer*, 140(February, 1971), cover, 21-27.
Interview with Cesar Chavez.

"Four Year Strike, Two Year Boycott: Showdown." *U.S. News*, 67(July 14, 1969), 83-84.
Boycott of table grapes getting results: 10 growers ask for contract talks.

Freeman, Roland. "Boycott Grapes." *Engage*, 2(November 15, 1969), 9-14.
Photographic essay: Chavez's visit to Washington, September 29-October 1, 1969.

Friedenberg, Edgar Z. "The Grape Workers' Strike." *New York Review*, 6(March 3, 1966), 10-12.

Friedland, William H. "Labor Waste in New York: Rural Exploitation and Migrant Workers." *Trans-Action*, 6(February, 1969), 48-53.

Friedman, Milton. "Migrant Workers." *Newsweek*, 76(July 27, 1970), 60.
Effects in Michigan of stricter federal and state standards for housing migrant farm workers. ". . . do-gooders responsible for this type of legislation . . ."

"From Delano to Sacramento." *America*, 114(April 2, 1966), 430.
Pilgrimage to Sacramento, March 17-April 10, 1966.

"From Fruit Bowl to Salad Bowl." *Time*, 96(September 14, 1970), 18.
Cesar Chavez and UFWOC move to organize workers in Salinas Valley

vegetable growing area; Teamsters; UFWOC contract with Inter-Harvest.

Fromm, Paul, "Fight This Organized Confusion." *Canada Month,* Vol. 9, No. 6(1969), 16-17.
California grape boycott.

Fry, John R. "No More Table Grapes Again!" *Christianity and Crisis,* 33(July 9, 1973), 137-139.

Fulco, Lawrence J. "How Mechanization of Harvesting Is Affecting Jobs." *Monthly Labor Review,* 92(March, 1969), 26-32.
Mechanization stimulated by increased labor costs, fewer foreign workers; P.L. 78, braceros.

Fuller, Varden. "Emerging Farm Labor Issues." *Farm Labor Developments,* January, 1967, pp. 26-34
Unionization, National Labor Relations Act, minimum wage.

———. "A New Era For Farm Labor?" *Industrial Relations,* 6(May, 1967), 285-302. Reprinted by Institute of Industrial Relations, University of California at Los Angeles, 1967. Reprint No. 307.
Termination of bracero program, possibilities for unionization.

"Future of Collective Bargaining in U.S. Agriculture," *Labour Gazette,* 68(December, 1968), 703-704.

Gagen, Joseph F. "Squeezing California's Grape Growers," *Commonweal,* 88(June 14, 1968), 374.

Galarza, Ernesto. "Big Farm Strike: A Report on the Labor Dispute at the DiGiorgio's." *Commonweal,* 48(June 4, 1948), 178-182.

Gallardo, Lloyd L. "The 'Green-carder'." *Employment Security Review,* 30(January, 1963), 25-27.

Garnett, Bernard E. "Chicano Migrant Workers Organize." *Race Relations Reporter,* 2(August 2, 1971), 5-6.
Study of living and working conditions; UFWOC.

Gersmehl, Glen. "The Vision of Cesar Chavez." *Christianity and Crisis.* 30(January 11, 1971), 296-300.
Interview with Jim Drake.

Gibbons, Richard P. "Farm Workers and City Unions." *New Republic,* 165(July 24 & 31, 1971), 12-13.
Farm Labor legislation [Senate Bill 371] in State of Washington supported by "peculiar alliance between growers and urban labor unions."

Gibbons, Russell W. Review of Matthiessen, *Sal Si Puedes. Ave Maria,* 111(March 7, 1970), 17-20.

Gibbons, Russell W. (Continued)

———. "The Teamsters." *Commonweal,* 98(August 10, 1973), 426-431.
Includes information on Teamster activities in farm labor organizing.

Gilmore, N. Ray and Gladys W. Gilmore. "The Bracero in California." *Pacific Historical Review,* 32(August, 1963), 265-282.
P.L. 78. Mentions AWOC, National Farmers Union, Teamsters, and greencarders.

Givens, Richard A. "Legal Disadvantages of Migratory Workers." *Labor Law Journal,* 16(September, 1965), 584-596.

———. "Report on Migratory Farm Labor." *Labor Law Journal,* 18(April, 1967), 246-248.
Advocates including farm workers under provisions of the National Labor Relations Act and broadening their coverage under the Fair Labor Standards Act.

Glass, Judith Chanin. "Organization in Salinas." *Monthly Labor Review,* 91(June, 1968), 24-27.
Workers in lettuce industry in California: various attempts at organization.

Goben, Ron. "Farm Workers Worry About Pesticide Poisons." *Canner/Packer,* 139 (February, 1970), 21-24.

Gomez-Q., Juan. "Research Notes on the Twentieth Century." *Aztlan,* 1(Spring, 1970), 115-132.

Grant, Allan. "California Grapes and the Boycottt—The Growers' Side of the Story." *Presbyterian Life,* 21(December 1, 1968), 20-21+. Also in *California Farm Bureau Monthly,* January, 1969.
Author is president of the California State Board of Agriculture and of the California Farm Bureau Federation.

———. "The Farm Worker: Needs More Than Unions." *Farm Quarterly,* 25(Spring Planning, 1970), 57+.
Part of a three-article series, "The Farm Worker:" The other two articles were written by William Kircher and Gavan Daws.

"Grape Boycott." *Church and Society,* 60(January-February, 1970), 66-67.

"Grape Boycott." *Monthly Labor Review,* 93(June, 1970), 80.
First contract with table grape growers: lists five ranches.

"The Grape Boycott." *Railway Clerk,* August 1, 1968. pp. 6-7.

"The Grape Boycott—Fair or Foul?" *Supermarketing,* 24(August, 1969), 15.
Editorial.

"Grape Boycott: Growers Say 'Grab the Ball and Run!'" *American Fruit Grower,* 89(April, 1969), 20+.

"Grape Boycott Hurting Sales." *Laborer*, 23(August, 1969), 12-13.

"Grape Boycott: Round 2." *New Republic*. 162(April 25, 1970), 10.
Union label grapes.

"Grape Boycott Still in Force." *America*, 120 (March 15, 1969), 291-292.
Newsnote: George Meany reaffirms AFL-CIO support; NLRA.

"Grape Harvest." *Economist*, 235(May 30, 1970), 48.
Signing of first contracts with table grape growers, grape boycott, National Conference of American Bishops, pesticides, California Rural Legal Assistance.

"Grape Pickers." *Monthly Labor Review*, 93(July, 1970), 79.
New three-year contract between UFWOC and Gallo Winery replaces the old contract signed in 1967.

"Grape Pickers Win Contract." *America*, 122 (April 18, 1970), 400.
News item: first contracts signed with three Coachella Valley growers.

"The Grape Strike." *Together*, September, 1966, p. 42.

"Grape Strikers Hail First Victory On 'Factory Farms'." *Catering Industry Employee*, 75(April, 1966), 12.
Schenley recognizes NFWA as collective bargaining agent.

"The Grape War." *Newsweek*, 81(May 21, 1973), 82-83.
Coachella Valley, grower-Teamster contracts.

"The Grape Workers of Delano." *UAW Solidarity*, 10(February, 1966), 16.

"Grapes and Wrath." *Campus Call*, October 27, 1968.
Interview with Lupe Anguiano of UFWOC's Michigan Boycott Office.

"Grapes of Wrath." *Christian Century*, 83 (*January 5, 1966*) 6.
Grape strike. Ad hoc committee of clergymen seeking Congressional investigation and new legislation for farm workers.

"Grapes of Wrath." *Christian Century*. 86(July 23, 1969), 1005.
Pentagon's increased purchases of California table grapes for shipment to Vietnam. Tongue-in-cheek report from a "captured Vietcong communique."

"Grapes of Wrath." *Newsweek*, 66(December 27, 1965), 57-58.
Strike in Delano; boycott of Schenley and DiGiorgio products.

"Grapes of Wrath." *Newsweek*, 76(August 3, 1970), 15.
Senate Subcommittee hearings on migrant labor.

"The Grapes of Wrath." *Scholastic Scope*, 6(February 24, 1967), 4-9.
Resume of Steinbeck's novel, followed by a description of the status of migrants today; NFWA; Chavez.

"Grapes of Wrath." *Time*, 86(December 10, 1965), 96.
Reverend Wayne Hartmire, Migrant Ministry.

"Grapes of Wrath: Freedom to Buy and Sell Is Perishable Too." *Barron's,* 48(August 5, 1968), 1.
Anti-boycott.

"Grapes of Wrath in California." *America,* 114(January 8, 1966), 33-34.
News item: support for strike by the clergy and by the UAW.

"Grapes of Wrath—New Style." *Economist,* 215(April 3, 1965), 52.

"Grapes Tabled." *Economist,* 231(June 28, 1969), 49-50.

"Grapestakes." *Nation's Agriculture,* 45(July/August, 1970), 19.
Contest, sponsored by the American Farm Bureau Federation and the California Table Grape Commission, offers prizes for eating California table grapes.

Gray, M. Laurel. "The Church During A Strike." *Lutheran Standard,* 7(August 22, 1967), 5-7+.
"Churches in the strike-ridden vineyard country of California find themselves in the middle of apparently conflicting interests of workers and owners."

"The Great Grape Controversy." *St. Anthony Messenger,* 76(December, 1968), 50.

Greene, Sheldon L. "Immigration Law and Rural Poverty—The Problem of the Illegal Entrant." *Duke Law Journal,* June, 1969, pp. 475-494.

———. "Wetbacks, Growers and Poverty." *Nation,* 209(October 20, 1969), 403-406.
Greencarders and illegal entries.

Gregor, Howard F. "The Large Industrialized American Crop Farm." *Geographical Review,* 60(April, 1970), 151-175.

Groom, Phyllis. "Report From the National Farm Labor Conference." *Monthly Labor Review,* 88(March, 1965), 275-278.

———. "Today's Farm Jobs and Farm Workers." *Monthly Labor Review,* 90(April, 1967), 1-5.
P.L. 78, UFWOC, Fair Labor Standards Act.

Gross, Robert A. "The Chicanos." *Newsweek,* 75(February 16, 1970), 96-98.
Comparative review and critique of Matthiessen, *Sal Si Puedes,* and Steiner, *La Raza.*

"Group Hits Texas Rangers for Anti-Labor Activities." *Seafarers Log,* 32(April, 1970), 13.
Texas Advisory Committee of the U.S. Civil Rights Commission; greencarders; federal and state legislation.

"Growers Face Loss of Braceros." *Business Week,* August 22, 1964, p. 120.
Impending expiration of P.L. 78.

Guzman, Ralph. "Mexican-Americans on the Move." *IUD Agenda,* 2(July, 1966), 3-8.
Living and working conditions of Mexican Americans, primarily in the Southwest; NFWA.

Haener, Al. "Profile of a Strike: Where the Grapes of Wrath Are Stored." *UAW Solidarity, 9* (December, 1965), 16.

Hallett, Douglas L. "Bitter Fruit in the Vineyards." *Nation's Business,* 58(February, 1970), 80-83.
Most workers do not want a union. UFWOC distorts picture of working and living conditions, wages. Author spent 5 days in Delano.

Harley, Ron. "The Furious Controversy Over New Farm Labor Laws." *Farm Quarterly,* 27(Fall, 1972), 26-27.
"Like the new laws in Arizona, Idaho and Kansas, the proposed California law [Proposition 22] would strip Cesar Chavez's United Farm Workers Union (UFWU) of its two most effective organizing weapons—the secondary boycott and the organizational strike."

———. "Labor Unrest in the Salad Bowl." *Farm Quarterly,* 25(November-December, 1970), 58-60.
Salinas Valley. UFWOC/Teamster "jurisdictional dispute" hurting growers. Salinas Valley Independent Growers Association (small and medium sized growers) formed to fight both unionization and large growers.

———. "Why They Signed With the Union." *Farm Quarterly,* 25(September-October, 1970), 56-58+.
Growers Bruno Dispoto and Hollis Roberts: "We could have eased all the damage done to an industry had we had earlier face-to-face communication with Chavez."

Harmer, Ruth. "Poisons, Profits and Politics." *Nation,* 209(August 25, 1969), 134-137.
Activities of UFWOC to control the use of pesticides by growers.

Harper, Robert G. "Mechanization and the Seasonal Farmworker." *Farm Labor Developments,* April, 1967, pp. 8-20.

Harris, Thomas E. "Some Remedies For an Aging NLRA." *American Federationist,* 78(February, 1971), 16-22.
Includes section on possible effects of application of NLRA to farm workers.

Hartmire, Wayne C., Jr. "Decision at Delano." *Town & Country Church,* 188(May-June, 1966), 3-6.

Hartmire, Wayne C., Jr.(Continued)

———. "Farm Workers on the Fringe." *Christian Century*, 81(July 29, 1964), 959-962.

———. "The Farm Workers' Struggle As Servanthood." *Metanoia*, 2(March, 1970), 8-9+.

———. "For California Farm Workers: It Is the Grape Boycott That Matters." *Migration Today*, No. 12(Spring, 1969), 13-22.
Background on Cesar Chavez, agribusiness, NFWA, UFWOC, Delano grape strike, and the role of the church.

———. "Help Your Brother." *Monday Morning*, March 23, 1970, pp. 6-7.

———. "Huelga!" *Southern California Presbyterian*, December, 1965, p. 9.
Arrest of pickets, including churchmen, in Delano; need for churches to become involved.

———. "The Mexican American Farmworker Fights For a Future." *Tempo*, 1(March 1, 1969), 6-7.
Background on Cesar Chavez, NFWA, UFWOC, Delano grape strike, agribusiness, and the role of the church.

———. "Ministry to Migrants." *Southern California Presbyterian*, March. 1963, pp. 8-9.
California Migrant Ministry and its work with migrant farm workers.

———. "The Plight of Seasonal Farm Workers." *Christianity and Crisis*. 25(October 4, 1965), 203-207.
P.L. 78, P.L. 414, braceros, labor legislation, Farm Workers Organization of Tulare County.

———. "The Real Story Behind the Grape Boycott." *Integrator*, 2(Spring, 1969), 20-21.

———. "Servanthood Among Seasonal Farm Workers—What Form?" *Presbyterian Life*, 22(March 1, 1969), 17-19+.
California Migrant Ministry, grape strike and boycott, living and working conditions.

"Harvest in the Vineyards." *Economist*, 219(April 16, 1966), 248.

"A Harvest Nears For Cesar Chavez." *Business Week*, June 27, 1970, p.62+.
Signing of contracts with several growers; increasing strength of UFWOC.

Hasiwar, Hank. "The Corporate Farmer: Agriculture's Newest Blight." *New Leader*, 35(January 21, 1952), 15-18.
National Agricultural Workers Union. "Hiring of 'wetbacks' makes it difficult for agricultural workers to organize."

Hawley, Ellis W. "The Politics of the Mexican Labor Issue, 1950-1965." *Agricultural History,* 40(July, 1966), 157-176.
Background and history of P.L. 78. Good notes and references.

Healy, Cletus. "Subversion in the Grape Industry." *The Truth About Communism,* Nos. 39-41 (1969). Milwaukee: Truth, Inc.
"And the involvement of the Soviet agents (and their dupes) in the Chavez operation deserves our attention—before they succeed, not after."

"Help Put a Stop to Anti-Consumer Boycotts." *American Fruit Grower,* 89(September, 1969), 6.

Henninger, Daniel. "And Now Lettuce." *New Republic,* 163(October 10, 1970), 9-11.
Strike in Salinas Valley; lettuce boycott.

Herhold, Robert M. "Clergy Group Intervenes For Chavez." *National Catholic Reporter,* 7(December 18, 1970), 1+.
Group of Catholic, Jewish, and Protestant clergymen offer to serve as mediators between UFWOC and Salinas Valley lettuce growers; Chavez serving jail sentence.

———. "Laborers in the Vineyard." *Christian Herald,* 93(August, 1970), 6+.

Herring, Elizabeth. "The Eighty-Seventh Congress Considers Migratory Farm Labor." *Social Action,* 28(May, 1962), 20-25.

Hertzberg, Hendrik. "Cesar Chavez in New York City." *WIN,* 5(November 15, 1969), 20-21.
Chavez's visit to New York City, October 1969.

Hill, Howard. "Interview With Chavez." *LSCRRC* (Law Students Civil Rights Research Council), 3(October, 1969), 1-3.

"Hispanic Americans and the Crisis in the Nation." *Social Progress,* 59(July/August, 1969), 50-60.

Hoffman, Pat. "Hear the Rally Cry." *The Church Woman,* 37(January, 1971), 20-24.

———. "Where's the Huelga Now." *Catholic Worker,* 37(July-August, 1971), 1+.

———. "Women in Huelga." *Response,* October, 1971.

Hogue, James L. "Protection For the Agricultural Worker." *Monday Morning,* February 9, 1970, p. 5.

Holt, James S. "Extending Jobless Pay to Farmworkers." *Manpower,* 3(December, 1971), 27-31.

———. "Some Implications of Collective Bargaining For Farm Workers." *Farm Economics,* September, 1970, [pp. 1-4]

"Hope For Migrant Workers." *Progressive,* 34(September, 1970), 7-8.
Help for the farm workers has come, not from Washington, but from the organizational efforts of the farmworkers themselves.

"House Bill on Minimum Wage." *America,* 114(June 11, 1966), 821.
Editorial comment: minimum wage for farm workers under the Fair Labor Standards Act.

"House Rejects Bracero Program." *Christian Century,* 80(June 12, 1963), 766.
House of Representative does not renew P.L. 78.

"How a Government Policy Conflicts." *Nation's Business,* 53(May, 1965), 33+.
Bracero program.

Howard, Al. "Delano: The General Strike in the Grapes." *Insurgent,* 2(January-February, 1966), 7-12.

"The Huelga—And Its Servants Unto Death." *California Crossroads,* 7(November, 1965), 7-12.
James Drake and Julio Hernandez address meeting of Unitarian Universalist Fellowship to explain the situation in Delano.

"Huelga! Tales of the Revolution." *Ramparts,* 5(July, 1966), 37-50.

"IAA Speaker Gives 'Inside' On Grape Strike." *American Fruit Grower,* 88(December, 1968), 9+.
John Giumarra, Jr. addresses International Apple Association convention.

"In Support of Farm Workers." *Illinois Church Councilor,* 33(February, 1969), 2-3.
Illinois Council of Churches votes to adopt the statement by the National Council of Churches supporting farm workers. Gives text of the NCC Statement.

"Interview With Cesar Chavez." *Catholic Worker,* 37(February, 1971), 1+.
El Malcriado interviews Chavez upon his release from jail, December, 1970.

"It Works!—Delano's Growing Service Center Fills Many New Functions."*IUD Agenda,* 4(January/February, 1968), 16-18.
The Farm Workers' Service Center.

Jacobs, Paul. "The Forgotton People." *Reporter,* 20(January 22, 1959), 12-20.
Migrant farm labor: braceros, P.L. 78, child labor.

———. Introduction to "Huelga! Tales of the Revolution." *Ramparts,* 5(July, 1966), 39.

———. "Man With a Hoe, 1964." *Commentary,* 38(July, 1964), 26-29.
Jacobs describes his experiences as a temporary migrant laborer in California.

Jacobs, Paul (Continued)

———. "A Matter of Spirit." *New Leader,* 44(October 2, 1961), 9-10.
AWOC's efforts to organize farm workers; AFL-CIO's decision to curtail financial support; Teamsters. Article is critical of AFL-CIO decision.

Jones, E. Walton. "Farm Labor and Public Policy." *Monthly Labor Review,* 91(March, 1968), 12-15.
South; minimum wage; legislation.

Jones, Lamar B. "Farm Labor: Shortage or Surplus." *Southwestern Social Science Quarterly,* 47(March, 1967), 401-412.

———. "Labor and Management in California Agriculture, 1864-1964." *Labor History,* 11(Winter, 1970), 23-40.
". . .presentation of the historical position of farm-management attitudes toward harvest labor. . . .the seeds of the present tensions in California were germinated in attitudes developed a century ago."

———. "Public Law 78 and Farm Manpower Problems." *Labor Law Journal,* 17(February, 1966), 83-88.

——— and James W. Christian. "Some Observations on the Agricultural Labor Market." *Industrial and Labor Relations Review,* 18(July, 1965), 527-529.

Keisker, Sue. "Harvest of Shame." *Commonweal,* 74(May 19, 1961), 202-205.
Farm workers, National Farmers Union, Farm Bureau, AFL-CIO organizing in California.

Kelley, Eugene A. and Arnold Mayer. "The 'Forgottenest'." *IUD Agenda,* 1(May, 1965), 5-9.
Migrant farm workers.

Kim, Chrysostom. "Cesar Chavez In Delano." *Worship,* 44(October, 1970), 488-496.

King, Lawrence T. "Bishops in the Vineyard." *Commonweal,* 92(May 15, 1970), 214.

———. "Pickets in the Valley." *Commonweal,* 73(October 14, 1960), 64-67.
AWOC, organization of farm workers in California.

———. "The Unjolly Green Giant." *Commonweal,* 86(July 28, 1967), 461.
Use of green-card workers in Imperial Valley opposed by merchants and domestic workers.

King, Patricia Z. "The Agricultural Minimum Wage in Low Wage Areas." *Farm Labor Developments,* May, 1968, pp. 21-28.

———. "Agricultural-Worker Coverage Under State Minimum Wage Laws." *Farm Labor Developments,* May, 1968, pp. 45-48.

Kircher, William. "The Farm Worker: Needs to Be Unionized." *Farm Quarterly,* 25(Spring Planning, 1970), 56+.
Part of a three-article series, "The Farm Worker:" The other two articles were written by Allan Grant and Gavan Daws. Kircher is Director of Organization. AFL-CIO.

Kirker, Sherwood. "Grapes and Morality." *UAW Solidarity,* 12(September, 1969), 8-9.
UAW support for grape boycott.

Knebel, Stanley M. "Federal Minimum Wage Protection For Farmworkers." *Farm Labor Developments,* September, 1966, pp. 23-25.

———. "Restrictive Admission Standards: Probable Impact on Mexican Alien Commuters." *Farm Labor Developments.* November, 1968, pp. 8-16.

Knoop, John G. "Strike, Boycott and Contract." *Farm Quarterly,* 21(Fall, 1966), 56-58+.
Chavez, NFWA, AWOC, Delano grape strike, Schenley boycott and contract, DiGiorgio elections.

Knutson, Ronald D. and Bernard L. Evans. "Organizational and Institutional Changes Needed in an Industrialized Agriculture: Bargaining, Unionization, Unemployment Insurance." *American Journal of Agricultural Economics,* 52(December, 1970), 790-791.

Kopkind, Andrew. "The Grape Pickers' Strike: A New Kind of Labor War in California." *New Republic,* 154(January 29, 1966), 12-15.
Background on Chavez, beginning of grape strike, AWOC, NFWA, end of bracero program, sources of support and opposition.

———. "Poverty Politics In California." *New Republic,* 156(February 18, 1967), 19-20.
OEO funds for California Center for Community Development; Chavez, grape strike.

Kostyu, Frank A. "Cesar Chavez: Poor, Dark and Burning With a Patient Fire." *United Church Herald,* 14(February, 1971), 45.

———. "Shadows in the Valley." *United Church Herald,* 11(August, 1968), 14-21.
Rio Grande Valley, Texas.

Koziara, Karen S. "Agricultural Minimum Wage: A Preliminary Look." *Monthly Labor Review,* 90 (September, 1967), 26-29.
Minimum wage for farm workers.

———. "Collective Bargaining on the Farm." *Monthly Labor Review,* 91(June, 1968), 3-9.

Krebs, A.V., Jr. "Agribusiness in California." *Commonweal,* 93(October 9, 1970), 45-47.

Growers receive large subsidies and exercise much economic and political control. Also mentions UFWOC, grape boycott, Bank of America.

———. "Anti-Chavez Worker Group Admits Its Industry Backing." *National Catholic Reporter,* 5(March 12, 1969), 1+.

Agricultural Workers Freedom to Work Association.

———. "Bishops Stay Out of the Vineyard." *Commonweal,* 89(December 20, 1968), 393-394.

———. "Bringing Democracy to America's Poor." *Ave Maria,* 110(August 23, 1969), 19-24.

———. "Bringing Democracy to the American Farm." *Pallatine Apostolate,* 6(December, 1967/January, 1968), 17-22.

———. "Cesar Chavez, Final Hope for California Farm Workers." *St. Anthony Messenger,* 76(August, 1968), 14-23, cover.

———. "Cesar Chavez: Huelga." *U.S. Catholic,* 32(September, 1966), 30-34.

———. "A Day in Delano." *Ave Maria,* 103(January 29, 1966), 8-10.

Delegation of national religious leaders attend fact-finding mission.

———. "Delano: Two Years After." *St. Joseph Magazine,* 68(October, 1967),

———. "Farm Union Fights DDT in California." *National Catholic Reporter,* 5(April 23, 1969), 5.

———. "Farm Workers and Labor Laws." *Extension,* 61(June, 1966), 16.

———. "Huelga." *Reign of the Sacred Heart,* 138(March, 1966), 2+.

———. "The Migrant Ministry." *Lamp,* 66(February, 1968), 22+.

———. "A New Taste For Grapes in Vietnam." *National Catholic Reporter,* October 9, 1968.

———. "Pesticides: Who Are We Killing." *U.S. Catholic and Jubilee,* 35(March, 1970), 23-26.

———. "The Second Gold Rush." *San Francisco,* February, 1970, pp. 24-25+.

Agribusiness in California.

Kucharsky, David E. "Grape Debate." *Christianity Today,* 13(October 11, 1968), 41-43.

"La Causa Chicana." *Social Caseworker.* 52(May, 1971), 259-334.

Entire issue devoted to various aspects of the Chicano movement. Includes articles and book reviews.

"La Huelga." *Monthly Labor Review,* 93(September, 1970), 58.
Signing of contract with twenty-six grape growers, July 29, 1970.

"Labor Comes to Life in the Grape Fields." *New Republic,* 154(April 23, 1966), 6-7.

"Labor In the Vineyards: The Boycott and the NLRA." *Nation,* 208(May 12, 1969), 591-593.
Grape strike and boycott; state and federal farm labor legislation.

"Labor, 1970." *Nation,* 211(September 7, 1970), 162-163.
Editorial: UFWOC success with grape growers; possiblities for other growers in California and elsewhere in the U.S.

LaBrucherie, Roger A. "Aliens in the Fields: The Green Card Commuter Under the Immigration and Naturalization Laws." *Stanford Law Review,* 21(June, 1969), 1750-1776.

Lane, Laura. "Why You Need a Farm Labor Law Now!" *Top Op*[erator], 3(June, 1971), 15-19.

Lantz, Jacob. "Oppression of the Hired Man." *Dimensions,* Summer 1969, pp. 29-32.
Support of the grape boycott by the Massachusetts Board of Rabbis.

Lara-Braud, Jorge. "America's Second Largest Minority." *Tempo,* 1(March 1, 1969), 4-5. Also published, under the title "The Second Largest Ethnic Minority in the U.S.A.," in *Migration Today,* No. 12(Spring, 1969), 5-12.

———. "La Raza Unida." *Social Progress,* 59(May-June, 1969), 8-10.

———. "Problems We Face In the Lower Rio Grande Valley." *Social Progress,* 59(May-June, 1969), 22-24.

———. "Report on Farm Labor Relations In the Lower Rio Grande Valley." Texas Council of Churches, *Texas Ecumenical Action,* May-June, 1967.

Leary, Mary Ellen. "As the Braceros Leave." *Reporter,* 32(January 28, 1965), 43-44.

———. "The Reagan Model." *Nation,* 212(February 1, 1971). 134-135.
Veto of OEO grant to California Rural Legal Assistance.

LeBlanc, Jerry. "The Bitter Grapes of Cesar Chavez." *Boston Sunday Globe,* May 25, 1969, pp. 30-34.

"Legislative Developments Affecting Farmworkers," *Farm Labor Developments,* March, 1966, pp. 39-41.

"Lettuce Grower Signs." *Monthly Labor Review,* 94(July, 1971), 68-69.
Contract between UFWOC and Mel Finerman Co. covers 5000 workers.

"Lettuce Settlement." *Monthly Labor Review,* 94(May, 1971), 75.
Agreement between UFWOC and Teamsters.

"Lettuce Strike." *Canadian Labour,* 16(January, 1971), 17.
National Farmers Union in Canada supports UFWOC lettuce boycott.

"Lettuce Strike." *Church and Society* [formerly *Social Progress*]. 61(November-December, 1970), 70-72.

"Lettuce Test." *Economist,* 237 (December 12, 1970), 56+.
Lettuce strike and boycott, Chavez's jail sentence, Teamsters, Dow Chemical, Bud Antle.

Lewis, D.C. "Farm Labor Unionization: Real Issues." *Agricultural Engineering,* 50(November, 1969), 669+.

Lewis, Norman. "Slave-Labourers in the Vineyard." *The Sunday Times Magazine* [London], February 1, 1970, 18-39.

Link, Terry. "UFWOC Sues For $10 Million." *National Catholic Reporter,* 7(February 5, 1971), 1+.

Lipson, James. "Victory." *Labor Today,* 9(May-June, 1970), 5-6.
First contract with table grape growers; federal subsidies for growers; various unions supporting UFWOC.

Lipton, Howard. "In Delano: A Companero Is Honored." *UAW Solidarity,* 12(October, 1969), 4-5.
UAW Ford Local leaders in Delano to support strike; UFWOC pays tribute to Roy Reuther.

"The Little Strike That Grew to La Causa." *Time,* 94(July 4, 1969), 16-21.

Livingston, John W. "Migrant Workers and Trade Unions." *American Federationist,* 67(February, 1960), 8-9.

Logsdon, G. "Fight for Farm Labor." *Farm Journal,* 90(March, 1966), 89.

———. "Wrath of Grapes." *Farm Journal,* 93(February, 1969), 33+.
Organizing farm labor.

Longcope, Kay. "The Changing Role of the Migrant Ministry." *Presbyterian Life,* 20(November 15, 1967), 12-16+.

"Long-Term Trends in Foreign-Worker Employment." *Farm Labor Developments,* February, 1968, 11-14.
Statistical report.

Lopez, Ronald W. "The El Monte Berry Strike of 1933." *Aztlan,* 1(Spring, 1970), 101-114.

"Los Mexicanos en Norteamerica: En Busca de una Identidad." *Economist para America Latina,* Vol. 2, No. 12(June 12, 1968), 16-18.
[In Spanish]. UFWOC, NFWA, Chavez, the grape strike; general conditions of migrant workers; Tijerina and "Brown Power."

Lyons, Daniel. "The Bishops' Poverty Program." *National Catholic Register.* May, 30, 1971.
UFWOC has collected more than enough money from its 50,000 dues-paying members and from donations and shouldn't have received a grant from the bishops' poverty fund.

———. "Chavez Bishops in Strange Predicament." *Twin Circle,* August 23, 1970, p. 2.
Opposes Bishops Committee position on farm workers' elections and inclusion under NLRA.

———. "Chavez Reaps Bitter Harvest." *Twin Circle,* July 12, 1970.
Criticizes Chavez, UFWOC, and the U.S. Bishops Ad Hoc Committee on the Farm Labor Dispute.

———. "Let's Clear Up the Confusion." *Twin Circle,* August 13, 1970, p.2.
Unionization of farm workers. The author favors the bill introduced by Senator George Murphy.

McBrearty, James C. "Harvest of Plenty in Fields of Shame: The Migrant Worker Today." *Arizona Review.* 20(February, 1971), 1-8.

MacCarry, Tim. "The Farmworkers' Struggle." *Catholic Worker,* 37(February, 1971), 3.
Review of London and Anderson, *So Shall Ye Reap.*

McCarthy, Charles A. "Diary of a Grape Strike." *Ave Maria,* 103(January 15, 1966), 19-22.
Chronology of grape strike, September 9-November 6, 1965.

"Machines Take Over Bracero Job." *Business Week,* January 8, 1966, pp. 108-110.

MacNabb, Betty L. "Texas Migrants Program: From Tax-eaters to Tax-Payers." *Communities In Action,* 2(March, 1967), 21-25.

McTaggart, Fred. "In Texas: A Time of Terror and Tears." *UAW Solidarity,* 10(July, 1967), 10-11.
UFWOC strike in Texas; Texas Rangers.

Maddocks, Lewis I. "Legislative Outlook in the 89th Congress: Domestic Issues." *Social Action,* 31(January, 1965), 4-15.
Section on migrant labor outlines various legislative needs.

Malone, Frank. "The Struggle to Organize the Farm Workers." *Arizona*, January 16, 1972, pp. 6-14.

"Manpower Implications of Fruit and Vegetable Mechanization—A Colloquium." *Farm Labor Developments*, December, 1969, pp. 1-6.
Report on the colloquium held at East Lansing, Michigan, July 21-23, 1969, sponsored by the Rural Manpower Center, Michigan State University.

"March of Migrants," *Life*, 60(April 29, 1966), 93-94.
Pilgrimage to Sacramento; Cesar Chavez and NFWA; Schenley boycott.

"Marcher." *New Yorker*, 43(May 27, 1967), 28.
Cesar Chavez.

Marshall, Patricia. "From Migrant Stream to Mainstream: 10-State Project Tests New Routes to Better Life For Itinerant Workers." *Manpower*, 3(July, 1971), 10-17.

Martin, Ray. "La Huelga: The Desperate Cry Along the Rio Grande." *UAW Solidarity*. 10(March, 1967), 3+.
Farm workers' strike in Texas.

Matthiessen, Peter. "Organizer: Profile of Cesar Chavez." *New Yorker*, Part 1, 45(June 21, 1969), 42-85; Part 2, (June 28, 1969), 43-71.

Maverick, Maury. "Marching For a Ghastly Recompense in Texas." *New Republic*, 155(September 24, 1966), 11.
Farm workers march from Rio Grande City to Austin, Texas.

Mayer, Arnold. "The Grapes of Wrath, Vintage 1961," *Reporter*, 24(February 2, 1961), 34-37.
Braceros: Congressional extension of P.L. 78.

Medina, Eliseo. "I Would Ask You Not to Eat At All." *Canner/Packer*, 138(February, 1969), 24+.
Remarks presented to the Chicago Council on Foreign Relations by UFWOC's Chicago grape boycott coordinator.

———. "The Most Powerful Weapon." *Labor Today*, 9(July-September, 1970), 16.
Grape boycott.

———. "Why a Grape Boycott." *Community*, Vol 28, No. 3(n.d.), 4-9.

Meister, Dick. "Grape Boycott." *Cosmopolitan*, 166(February, 1969), 50.

———. "La Huelga Becomes La Causa: California Grape Pickers Strike." *New York Times Magazine*, November 17, 1968, 52-53+.

———. "Still in Dubious Battle." *Nation*, 191(September 24, 1960), 178-180.
AWOC, AFL-CIO unionizing farm workers in California.

"Melon Growers—Next Target?" *American Vegetable Grower,* 18(August, 1970), 8.

"Methodists Urge Legislators to Solve Boycott Controversy." *California Farmer,* 230(January 18, 1969), 8+.

"The Mexican American in Texas." *Home Missions,* 38(July, 1967), 6+.

"Migrant Farm Workers Are Among Forgotten Americans." *Seafarers Log,* 32(August, 1970). 4.

"Migrant Labor in Upstate New York." *Columbia Journal of Law and Social Problems,* 4(March 27, 1968).

"Migrant Revolution." *Saturday Review,* 51(September 7, 1968), 29.
Letters to the editor in response to article by R. Tobin (August 17, 1968).

"The Migratory Farm Worker." *Monthly Labor Review,* 91(June, 1968), 10-12.

Miller, Ed S. "Stouffer Inn Gets Sermon on Unionism." *Catering Industry Employee,* 78(August, 1969), 1-4.

Miller, Judea B. "Delano Diary." *Midstream,* 15(March, 1969), 49-60.

Miller, M. Vincent. "Workers on the Farm: After the Grape Pickers' Strike." *Dissent,* 13(November-December, 1966), 645-655. Reprinted in Jeremy Larner and Irving Howe, eds., *Poverty: Views From the Left.* New York: William Morrow & Company, 1968, pp. 207-220.

Miller, Mike. "The Strike in the Grapes." *Commission on Religion and Race Reports,* 2(May, 1966).
Chavez and beginnings of NFWA, AWOC, grape strike, Schenley boycott, Pilgrimage to Sacramento.

Miller, Paul B. and John M. Glasgow. "Job Crisis Along the Rio Grande." *Monthly Labor Review,* 91(December, 1968), 18-23.
High unemployment among farm workers in South Texas; P.L. 78, braceros.

Mills, Nicolaus C. "Eagle Over the Lettuce Fields." *Commonweal,* 93(November 6, 1970), 140-141.
UFWOC efforts to organize lettuce workers complicated by grower-Teamster contracts and by court injunction against UFWOC.

———. "Greening the Pentagon." *New Leader,* 54(March 8, 1971), 4.
Pentagon increases purchases of Bud Antle lettuce.

———. "United Farm Workers vs. the NLRB." *Commonweal,* 96(April 28, 1972), 180-181.

———. "The Whip and the Bee: Diary From the Grape Strike." *Dissent,* 20(Spring, 1973), 200-205.

Mills, Nicolaus C. (Continued)

———. "Workers On Farms." *New Republic,* 157(September 23, 1967), 9.
Almaden and Perelli-Minetti contracts; agreement between UFWOC and Teamsters; strike against Giumarra Vineyards.

"Misery on the Move." *Economist,* 225(December 30, 1967), 1292.
Migrant labor.

Mitchell, H.L. "Blood on the Fruit." *American Federationist,* 55(June, 1948), 4-5.
DiGiorgio strike, 1948.

Moley, Raymond. "Bracero Blunder." *Newsweek,* 66(July 19, 1965), 88.
Government should not have allowed P.L. 78 to expire.

Monahan, W.J. "Vanishing Bracero." *Farm Chemicals,* 128(January, 1965), 40-41.

Moore, Joan W. and Ralph Guzman. "New Wind From the Southwest." *Nation,* 202(May 30, 1966), 645-648.
Problems of Mexican-Americans in the U.S., primarily five southwestern states. Mentions Chavez, the Delano grape strike, Community Service Organization, and the Mexican G.I. Forum.

Moore, Truman. "Slaves For Rent: The Shame of American Farming." *Atlantic,* 215(May, 1965), 109-122. Discussion and commentary, *Atlantic,* 216(July, 1965), 28, and 216(August, 1965), 34-36.
Study of the conditions under which migrant workers live and work throughout the country. Based on Moore's book, *The Slaves We Rent.*

"More Grapes of Wrath." *California Farmer,* 230 (January 18, 1969), 8D+.

"More Grapes of Wrath." *Economist,* 227(June 8, 1968), 54+.
Farm workers, braceros, minimum wage, UFWOC, merger of AWOC and NFWA, DiGiorgio, Schenley, Cesar Chavez, Starr County/Rio Grande Valley, Texas.

Morin, Roland. "Canada's Flag Carried Into the Grapefields of Delano." *UAW Solidarity,* 12(July, 1969), 6+.
Delegation from Canada, including UAW Canadian Region Director Dennis McDermott, visit striking UFWOC farm workers.

Morris, Austin P. "Agricultural Labor and National Labor Legislation." *California Law Review,* Berkeley, California, 54(December, 1966), 1939-1989.

———. "Of Many Things: The Rights of Agricultural Labor to Organize and Bargain Collectively." *America,* 118(January 13, 1968), inside cover.

Moyer, John R. "Cesar Chavez and the California Migrant Ministry." *Church in Metropolis,* 17(Summer, 1968), 14.

Moyer, John R. (Continued)

———. "A Conversation With Cesar Chavez." *Journal of Current Social Issues*, 3(November-December, 1970), 3-9.
Interview with Chavez.

———. "The United Farm Workers: A Translation of American Idealism." *Journal of Current Social Issues*. 10(Autumn, 1972), 23-27.

Muñoz, Marcos. "Progress For United Farm Workers." *NEGM Magazine*, June, 1970, p.8.

Murphy, Betty. "Community Development: 'There Aren't Any Miracles'." *Vista Volunteer*, 4(January, 1968), 12-19.
Two Vista volunteers working in California interview Cesar Chavez. Background on Chavez, Community Service Organization, and UFWOC.

Nabakov, Peter. "Taking the Lid Off." *Progressive*, 34(July, 1970). 40-41.
Review of Steiner's *La Raza* and Matthiessen's *Sal Si Puedes*.

"NAFC Ads Blast Grape Boycott." *Progressive Grocer*, 48(May, 1969), 112.

"Negotiating For Health." *Labor Today*, 9(May-June, 1970), 7-8.
Health and Safety clause in UFWOC contracts provides for control of use of various pesticides and other chemicals.

Nelkin, Dorothy. "Unpredictability and Life Style in a Migrant Labor Camp." *Social Problems*, 17(Spring, 1970), 472-487.

Nelson, Eugene, Jr. "Huelga: New Goals For Labor." *Nation*, 204(June 5, 1967), 724-725.
Discusses UFWOC strike in California and the need to organize farm workers in other states.

"New Farm Labor Agreement." *Monthly Labor Review*, 96(May, 1973), 64.
Agreement between Teamsters and National Farm Labor Contractors Association.

"New Grape Boycott Urged." *Christian Century*, 90(May 2, 1973), 503.
Grower-Teamster contracts in Coachella Valley.

"New Grapes." *Newsweek*, 70(July 31, 1967), 79.
El Teatro Campesino (Farm Workers Theater): description of a performance.

"Newcomer Wins On the Farm." *Business Week*, September 10, 1966, p. 158.
UFWOC wins bargaining agent election at DiGiorgio; merger of NFWA and AWOC.

Nix, James. "Effect of Cotton Harvest Mechanization on Hired Seasonal Labor." *Employment Security Review*, 30(January, 1963), 12-15.

"Nixon Plan For Farm Labor." *America*, 120(May 24, 1969), 606.

Editorial comment: Nixon wants Agricultural Board, not NLRB. No strike, no secondary boycott.

"Nixon Plan For Farm Workers." *U.S. News*, 66(May 19, 1969), 110-111.

Proposes creation of a Farm Labor Relations Board; would prohibit consumer boycottts and strikes.

"A Nonviolent Union." *Catholic Worker*, 34(March, 1968), 1+.

UFWOC.

Noonan, Joe, "Tips on Tactics in the Lettuce War." *National Catholic Reporter*, 7(November 27, 1970), 17.

Norris, Murray. "Delano Farm Workers Rally to Block Harrassment." *California Farmer*, 229(July 6, 1968), 8-9.

Agricultural Workers Freedom to Work Association, Gilbert Rubio, Jose Mendoza.

Novak, Michael. "The Grape Strike." *Commonweal*, 83(December 24, 1965), 366-369.

Background information; strike issues.

———. "The Grape Strike." *Concern*, 9(February 1, 1966), 54. 1966),6.

"Now They Walk With Us." *Newsweek*, 68(September 12, 1966), 54.

Texas strike; march from Rio Grande City to Austin.

O'Connell, Timothy J. "Lettuce Boycott Reaches New York," *America*, 124(Feburary 13, 1971), 148-149.

Chavez, UFWOC, lettuce boycott, nonviolence, pesticides, NLRA. UFWOC files suit against Pentagon; held rally in New York City to dramatize boycott and lawsuit.

Ogle, Alice. "California Farm Labor." *America*, 111(December 19, 1964), 799+.

Ending of importation of braceros under P.L. 78 and possible substitutes to be used by growers, including the use of welfare recipients and importing foreign workers under Section H-2 of the Immigration and Nationality Act (P.L. 414).

———. "Farm Labor, 1967." *Ave Maria*, 106(August 12, 1967), 18+.

———. "Farm Labor: USA." *Ave Maria*, 102(September 11, 1965), 5-8.

———. "Farm Workers Seek Laws That Don't Materialize." *National Catholic Reporter*, 4(January 3, 1968), 10.

———. "Huelga: Grape Pickers Strike in Delano, California." *Marriage*, 48 (May, 1966), 25-29.

———. "Mississippi West'." *New City*, February, 1966, pp. 18-20.

Delano, AWOC-NFWA.

———. "The Plight of Migrant America." *America*, 115(July 9, 1966), 33-34.

NFWA. Chavez, braceros' and migrant workers' living and working conditions throughout the country.

Ogle, Alice [*Continued*]
———. "Revolution in the Vineyards." *America,* 113(December 11, 1965), 747-748.
"Old Myth Fades." *Nation,* 201(July 19, 1965), 31.
Myth that cheap imported labor is necessary to save the crops.
"On the Bench: Domestic Farm Workers." *New Republic,* 153(August 7, 1965), 8.
"On the Road to Power." *Economist.* 227(June 8, 1968), 59-60.
Alianza Federal de Mercedes (Federal Alliance of Land Grants), Reies Lopez Tijerina, Cesar Chavez, La Raza.
"Oppressive Child Labor Practices—A Possible Solution." *St. Anthony Messenger,* 79(February, 1972), 15.
Editorial. Child labor in agriculture: legislation.
"The Orchardist and the Laborer Have No Choice." *American Fruit Grower,* 92(June, 1972), 36.
Editorial.
"Organized Labor's Stand on Migrant Problems." *American Child,* 40(January, 1958), 7-8.
O'Rourke, Edward W. "Union Labels on Grapes." *Catholic Rural Life,* 19(September, 1970), 2. Also published, under the title "United Farm Workers and the California Strike," in the *Catholic Post.* September 6, 1970, p. 6.
Editorial. UFWOC contracts with table grape growers and the role of the U.S. Bishops Ad Hoc Committee on the Farm Labor Dispute. Also discusses opposition by the Catholic weekly. *Twin Circle;* propects for federal legislation; and the need for unionization in other states with large numbers of farm workers.
Ortego, Philip D. "The Chicano Renaissance." *Social Casework,* 52(May, 1971), 294-307.
Renaissance "in literature, journalism, and drama."
———. "The Minority on the Border: Cabinet Meeting in El Paso." *Nation,* 205(December 11, 1967), 624-627.
Mexican/American affairs; LBJ-Diaz Ordaz meeting; Chavez, Tijerina.
Osborne, John. "The Poor Betrayed." *New Republic,* 164(February 13, 1971), 13-15.
California Rural Legal Assistance. OEO cuts funding after Governor Reagan vetoes grant.
"Our Best Hope." *Engage,* 2(November 15, 1969), 4-8.
Interview with Cesar Chavez. "Our best hope is the boycott . . . [and] people." Discusses greencard workers. Mexican and Filipino culture, voter registration, pesticides, the role of churches, and nonviolence.

"Our Blue-Sky Sweatshops." *Advance,* 57(June 11, 1971), 8-9.
Child labor in agriculture.

"Packing Shed Workers Respond to Teamster Organizing Campaign." *International Teamster,* 63(February, 1966), 4-6.
"The plan outlined by [Teamster Vice President George Mock] . . . is for the AWOC to organize the field workers and the Teamsters to unionize the packing shed and equipment operators."

Padilla, Gilbert. "Farm Workers Need Bargaining Rights." *Labor Today,* 6(August-September, 1967), 2-5.
Describes conditions in Starr County, Texas.

Palmer, L.M. "Grape Fight Spreads to Other Crops." *Farm Journal,* 94(September, 1970), 22.

Paul, Gordon W. "Michigan Farm Labor Management and the Migrant Worker." *Michigan State Economic Record,* 10(March, 1968), 1-2+.

"Pentagon Scabs." *Ramparts,* 7(November 30, 1968), 12+.

"Perseverence and Purity Pay Off For Chavez." *Christian Century,* 87(August 12, 1970), 956.
News item: signing of contract with grape growers.

"Pesticides and Birth Defects: Migrant Worker's Baby Is Center of New Probe." *UAW Solidarity,* 9(April, 1966), 13.

Peters, Kenneth W. "A Time For Harvesting." *Ave Maria,* 107(June 22, 1968), 6-10+.
Grape strike and boycott, greencarders, Chavez's fast for nonviolence, mechanization.

Phillips, Norman D. "Chicano Workers, Rio Grande Farmers Agree To Meet." *Christian Century,* 88(January 20, 1971), 84-86.
Rio Grande Valley small farmers agree to meet with farm workers under the auspices of the Texas Conference of Churches, Mentions UFWOC, Cesar Chavez, and Antonio Orendain.

"Pickets—and Purpose." *Newsweek,* 56(July 11, 1960), 76.
AWOC strike in San Joaquin Valley.

Pickett, Carleton I. "The Folly of Grape Throwing." *New England Farmer,* September, 1968, p. 5.

Pickett, Jack. "One-Year Extension Is A Disaster." *California Farmer,* 220(January 4, 1964), 4.
Editorial. Extension for one year of the bracero program (P.L. 78) is insufficient. " . . . the need for stoop labor [will] increase in California."

Pickett, Jack [*Continued*]

———. "Pickett Joins the Secret Service." *California Farmer,* 221(November 21, 1964), 114.

Describes "cloak-and-dagger" tactics necessary in order to import laborers from Mexico under P.L. 414, as opposed to the simplicity, for the growers, of P.L. 78.

"The Plan of Delano." *Catholic Mind,* 64(June, 1966), 20-22.

"Plight of Lettuce Eaters." *Time,* 100(September 18, 1972), 20-21.

"Plight of the Migrant Farmer." *Catholic Digest,* 33(February, 1969), 120-127.

Politzer, Jerome, "Cesar's Salad," *Christianity Today.* 15(January 1, 1971), 38-39.

Chavez's jail sentence, lettuce boycott, Dow, Antle, Teamsters. Church involvement. Ford Foundation grant to National Farmworkers Service Centers.

Pontier, Raymond J. "The California Grape Dispute." *The Church Herald,* December 13, 1969, pp. 10+.

Background of grape boycott; aims of UFWOC; supporting resolution of the Christian Action Commission of the Reformed Church in America.

Post, Don. "Mexican Americans and 'La Raza'." *Christian Century,* 86(March 5, 1969), 325-328.

"Prîvileged Entry Onto Farm Property For Union Organizers." *Hastings Law Journal,* 19(January, 1968), 413.

"The Prospects For Mechanizing the Strawberry Harvest." *Farm Labor Developments,* June, 1969, pp. 16-18.

Prosten, Dick. "Coming: 'Conglomerates' On the Farm." *IUD Agenda,* 4(January/February, 1968), 26.

The big conglomerate corporation farm; agribusiness.

Pryor, Alton. "Chavez in Coachella," *California Farmer,* 229 (July 6, 1968), 4.

Rapoport, Roger. "The Fox and the Grapes." *Los Angeles Times WEST Magazine,* November 23, 1969, pp. 13-18.

Cesar Chavez and the grape strike and boycott; viewpoints of growers and strikers.

Rasmussen, Barbara. "Legal Challenge to Rural Power." *IUD Agenda,* 4(May, 1968), 13-15.

California farm workers; California Rural Legal Assistance.

R[azee], D[on]. "The Grape Boycott: Past, Present, Future." *California Farmer,* 230(January 18, 1969), 5.

Razee, Don. "Agricultural Work is Unfit, CRLA Contends." *California Farmer,* 228(May 18, 1968).
California Rural Legal Assistance.

———. "Another Union Gets Into the Farm Labor Act." *California Farmer,* 220(June 6, 1964), 11.
Distillery Workers Union (AFL-CIO) contemplating organizing sugar beet workers.

———. "Boycott Jeopardizes Entire Grape Crop." *California Farmer,* 229(July 6, 1968), 7+.
Table grape boycott: adverse effects on growers.

"Recommendations of the California Farm Labor Panel." *Monthly Labor Review,* 88(December, 1965), 1413.
Public Law 78, braceros.

"Relevance of Nonviolence to Our Time." *People's Action* 4(February, 1970). 13-19.
Interviews with delegates, including James Drake of UFWOC, to the international seminar on the "Relevance of Gandhi to Our Times."

"Religious Leaders' Statement On Grape Pickers' Strike." *Ave Maria,* 103(January 29, 1966), 18.

"Rendering Unto Cesar." *Pacific Business,* March-April, 1971, pp. 33-39.
Interview with Daryl Arnold, President of the Free Marketing Council. Discusses UFWOC contracts.

Rendon, Armando. "How Much Longer the Long Road?" *Civil Rights Digest,* 1(Summer, 1968), 34-44.
Farm labor. Legislation, wages, UFWOC, Cesar Chavez, grape strike and boycotts, mechanization, strike in Texas, and migrants in New Jersey.

———. "La Raza—Today Not Manana." *Civil Rights Digest,* 1(Spring, 1968), 7-17.
Discusses the Cabinet Committee hearings on Mexican American Affairs and the La Raza Unida Conference, both of which took place in El Paso, October 1967.

"Report On Our Migrant Workers," *America,* 114(March 12, 1966), 346.
Editorial: Willard Wirtz, braceros.

Richardson, Lincoln. "Cesar Chavez." *Presbyterian Life,* 21(October 1, 1968), 16-19+.
Background on Chavez, UFWOC, grape strike and boycott, and unionization of farm workers.

"Rights For Farm Workers," *America,* 120(April 26, 1969), 492-493.

Editorial: boycott, UFWOC suit against Agricultural Workers Freedom to Work Association, NLRA coverage for farm workers.

Roberts, Steven V. Review of Matthiessen, *Sal Si Puedes*. *New York Times Book Review*, February 1, 1970, p. 8.

Rogers, Harold T. "Democrats Endorse Pro-UFW Plank." *American Fruit Grower*, 92(August, 1972), 17.

———. "Grape Boycott: It Affects All of Us." *American Fruit Grower*, 89(March, 1969), 11-14.

———. "A Lot of Lettuce." *American Fruit Grower*, 93(February, 1973), 34. Damage suits filed by UFW against Teamsters and a number of California growers; California Supreme Court ruling that "there was no jurisdictional dispute."

———. "Minute-Maid Signs." *American Fruit Grower*, 92(April, 1972), 42. UFW contract with Minute Maid division of Coca Cola; pending NLRB ruling on boycott.

———. "On the Labor Front." *American Fruit Grower*, 89(November, 1969), 6-7.
UFWOC; pesticides.

———. "On the Labor Front." *American Fruit Grower*, 90(August, 1970), 10. Contracts between UFWOC and table grape growers.

———. "On the Labor Front." *American Fruit Grower*, 90(September, 1970), 12-13.
"Grape growers may have signed contracts but there still are a lot of questions to be answered."

———. "UFW Calls Off Winery Boycott in Stall Tactic." *American Fruit Grower*, 92(May, 1972), 28-29.

———. "UFW Takes 'Detour': Lettuce Target Again." *American Fruit Grower*, 92(June, 1972), 23.

———. "UFWOC Recognized As Union." *American Fruit Grower*, 92(March, 1972), 66.

———. "Union Free-For-All." *American Fruit Grower*, 93(June, 1973), 38-39. UFW, Teamsters, grape contracts, Coachella Valley.

———. "You Can't Afford to Stand Alone." *American Fruit Grower*, 90(May, 1970), 11-12+.
Growers need legislation to help solve farm labor problems.

Romano, Octavio I. "The Anthropology and Sociology of Mexican-Americans: The Distortion of Mexican-American History," *El Grito*, 2(Fall, 1968), 13-26.

Ross, Livie. "Grape Workers Win New Gains," *Labor Today*, 5(August-September, 1966), 23-24+.

———. "Viva La Huelga!" *Labor Today*, 5(June-July, 1966), 23-24.
UAW Convention pledges support to NFWA and AWOC.

Roth, Norman. "Viva La Causa! Viva La Huelga!" *Labor Today*, 8(March, 1969), 3-7.
Interview with Eliseo Medina, UFWOC Chicago coordinator.

Rowan, Helen. "A Minority Nobody Knows." *Atlantic*, 219(June, 1967), 47-52.
Primarily about Mexican Americans in urban ghettos but mentions Cesar Chavez.

Roysher, Martin and Douglas Ford. "California's Grape Pickers Will Soon Be Obsolete." *New Republic*, 158(April 13, 1968), 11-12. Reply and rejoinder, W. Johnson, *New Republic*, 158(May 18, 1968), 40-41.
Mechanical harvester developed by University of California, Davis.

Rudick, Jeff. "Workers on the Land." *Catholic Worker*, 36(March-April, 1970), 1+.
UFWOC, grape strike and boycott.

Rummel, Charles A. "Current Developments in Farm Labor Law." *Labor Law Journal*, 19(April, 1968), 230-240.
Discussion of National Labor Relations Act, Fair Labor Standards Act, Labor Management Relations (Taft-Hartley) Act. Author is General Counsel of the California Farm Bureau Federation.

"Rural Worker In America." *Monthly Labor Review*, 91(June, 1968), Special section; iii-iv, 1-32.
Includes articles on Delano, the grape strike, and problems of farm workers.

Salandini, Victor. "Breakthrough in Coachella Valley." *America*, 122(May 2, 1970), 470-471.
Signing of first contracts with table grape growers; background on the grape strike.

———. "Cesar Chavez—A Controversy." *The Catholic Voice*, October 4, 1967, p. 11.

———. "Decision at DiGiorgio." *America*, 115(October 8, 1966), 415-418.
DiGiorgio election; UFWOC/Teamsters.

———. "The Delano Strike." *Commonweal*, 83(March 18, 1966), 683.
Letter to the editor.

———. "Lessons of the Grape Strike." *America*, 123(October 17, 1970), 285-287.

Salandini, Victor [*Continued*]

———. "More Grapes of Wrath." *America,* 119(August 17, 1968), 104-105.
Violence against pickets; table grape boycott.

———. Review of John Dunne, *Delano. Commonweal,* 87(February 9, 1968), 567-568.

———. "Syndicalisme et Solidarite Humaine: le Boycottage des Raisins de Table de Californie." *Relations,* No. 348(April, 1970), 117-118.

———. "Union Organizing in the Fields." *America,* 113(October 9, 1965), 400-401.
AWOC, AFL-CIO; braceros, P.L. 78.

Sanderson, R.K. and E.L. Barr, Jr. "Why Grape Growers Do Not Render Unto Cesar." *Christian Century,* 86(June 11, 1969), 810-811.

Sawyer, George. "The Great Grape Boycott." *Pacific: California Business Magazine,* November-December, 1968, pp. 13+.
California Chamber of Commerce opposition to grape boycott.

"Schenley Surrenders." *Christian Century,* 83(April 27, 1966), 515-516.

Schirber, Martin E. "The Migrant Worker." *American Benedictine Review,* 21(March, 1970), 56-78.

Schlossberg, Steve. "Harvest of Cheer." *UAW Solidarity,* 11(March, 1968), 13.
Judge orders rehiring of farm workers who were fired for joining UFWOC.

Schuck, Peter. "Tied to the Sugar Lands." *Saturday Review,* 55(May 6, 1972), 36-42.
Farm workers in Louisiana: living and working conditions; wages controlled by U.S. Department of Agriculture under provisions of the Sugar Act; possibilities for unionization.

Schwartz, Harry. "Organizational Problems of Agricultural Labor Unions." *Journal of Farm Economics,* 23(May, 1941), 456-466.
Problems are organization, finances, and leadership. Discusses the rise and decline of the Industrial Workers of the World (IWW), Cannery and Agricultural Workers Union, Sharecroppers Union of Alabama, Southern Tenant Farmers Union, and the United Cannery, Agricultural, Packing and Allied Workers. Includes a chart showing the number of agricultural strikes, 1927-1939.

———. "Recent Developments Among Farm Labor Unions." *Journal of Farm Economics,* 23(November, 1941), 833-842.
United Cannery, Agricultural, Packing and Allied Workers; AFL Federal Labor Unions; Teamsters; Federated Agricultural Laborers Association; Southern Tenant Farmers Union. " . . . the relative failure of these agricultural labor unions . . . ."

"Seething Vineyards." *Newsweek*, 72(July 8, 1968), 62.
Boycott of table grapes; UFWOC strike in Coachella Valley.

Segal, Aaron. "Mexico and the Mexican-American." *Con Safos*, Vol. 2, No. 5(1970), 16-20.
Discusses a number of topics, including migrant labor and green-card workers.

"A Self-Regulation Program For Agricultural Employers." *Farm Labor Developments*, October, 1969, pp. 8-9.
Program of the California Farm Bureau Federation for compliance with federal, state, and local laws covering farm workers. Among the areas in which they are urging compliance or recommending guidelines are payroll and employment records, sanitary facilities, drinking water, and pesticides control. "In order to gain popular support, the Federation feels that it must strive to keep agriculture above rebuke."

Selvin, David F. "The Rise of a Farm Workers Union." *American Federationist*, 74(May, 1967), 1-5.
AWOC, NFWA, beginning of grape strike, UFWOC, Schenley and DiGiorgio contracts, agribusiness, P.L. 78, mechanization, state and federal legislation.

"Senators in Our Fields," Citizens For Farm Labor, *Farm Labor*, 4(April, 1966), 7-17.
Hearings of the Senate Subcommittee on Migratory Labor, March 1966. Includes the statement submitted by Citizens For Farm Labor.

Shannon, James P. "Grape Pickers Put the Squeeze on Growers." *Our Sunday Visitor*, 57(September 22, 1968).

Sherrill, Robert G. "Agribusiness: Reaping the Subsidies." *Nation*, 209(November 24, 1969), 561-566.
Section on the activities of Cesar Chavez and UFWOC against the use of pesticides.

Sherry, Gerard E. "Biggest Lettuce Producer Signs With Chavez Union." *National Catholic Reporter*, 7(May 7, 1971), 3.

———. "Cesar Chavez." *Our Sunday Visitor*, 57(September 1, 1968), 10-11.

———. "Chavez Still Fasting, Gets Court Continuance." *National Catholic Reporter*, 4(March 6, 1968), 4.

Shuman, Charles B. "Grapes . . . And the Chain Store Boycott." *Nation's Agriculture*, September, 1968.

———. "Grapes Are Beautiful." *Nation's Agriculture*, 45(July/August, 1970), 4.

Grape boycott. The "ultimate objective [of the AFL-CIO] is to force every farm operator in America to pay union dues." The author was president of the American Farm Bureau Federation.

Silverman, Mark. "Grape Boycott." *Catholic Worker*, July-August, 1969, p. 6.

Simmons, Robert. "Sending a Boy To Do a Job You Wouldn't Even Wish On a Man." *Today's Health*, 49(July, 1971), 44-49.
Child labor in agriculture.

Sinisi, Joseph S. "Boycott: UFWOC Digs In For Long Struggle." *Supermarketing*, 25(November, 1970), 20+.

" 'A Skunk Is a Skunk'." *Nation*, 212(June 14, 1971), 740.
Farm Labor Service.

Social Progress, 59(May-June, 1969), 3-47.
Issue devoted to problems of Mexican Americans. Includes several relevant articles.

Solis, Faustina. "Socioeconomic and Cultural Conditions of Migrant Workers." *Social Casework*, 52(May, 1971), 308-315.

Spiegel, W.H. "Trade Unions in Agriculture." *Rural Sociology*, 6(June, 1941), 117-125.

"Spragg and Delegation Support Jailed Chavez." *United Church Herald*, 14(February, 1971), 8.

Stanford, John W. "Viva La Huelga!" *Political Affairs*, 46(August, 1967), 22-32.
Strike in Texas; background of UFWOC.

Stanley, Harold F. "Mechanization and the Recruitment of Farm Workers." *Farm Labor Developments*, August, 1968, pp. 11-23.
Covers a number of different crops in different areas of the country.

Stark, Rodney, *et al.* "Sounds of Silence." *Psychology Today*, 3(April, 1970), 38-41.
Survey of Protestant ministers in California inquiring whether or not they have given sermons on controversial moral, ethical, or political issues, among them the grape strike.

"Statement On Farm Labor By the U.S. Bishops, Washington, D.C., November, 1968" *Catholic Mind*, 67(January, 1969), 4-6.

Steiner, Stan. "The Cultural Schizophrenia of Luis Valdez." *Vogue*, March 15, 1969, pp. 112-113+.
El Teatro Campesino.

———. "No One Hears Our Silence." *Progressive*, 34(May, 1970), 37-39.
Organizing farm workers in Arizona.

Stewart, Clifford A. "The Shame of American Agriculture." *Focus/Midwest*, Vol. 3, No. 4(n.d.), 14-15.

Stiles, B.J., "Who Spiked the Grapes." *Christianity and Crisis*, 29(October 27, 1969), 272-274.
Use of pesticides by growers; purchase of grapes by the Defense Department; Chavez; UFWOC; grape boycott.

"Stoop Labor." *Commonweal*, 81(February, 5, 1965), 596-597.
California growers miss "abundant supply of docile, cheap and efficient Mexican labor."

"Stoop Labor Furor: Bracero System." *Senior Scholastic*, 86(May 6, 1965), 18-19.

"Stooping To Conquer." *Newsweek*, 67(February 7, 1966), 61-62.
Secretary of Labor Wirtz report, *Year of Transition:* "The false notion that Americans won't do stoop labor was carefully nurtured from the truer fact that they won't work for stoop wages."

Sufrin, Sidney C. "Labor Organization in Agricultural America, 1930-1935." *American Journal of Sociology*, 43(January, 1938), 544-559.

Sullivan, John R. "Sponsor Predicts Success For Farm Union Legislation." *National Catholic Reporter*, 4(February 14, 1968), 2.

"Summer Brings the Mexicans: The National Farm Labor Union (AFL) Discusses the Importation of Mexican Agricultural Laborers." *Commonweal*, 48(July 2, 1948), 275-278.
Discusses the provisions of the agreement between the Mexican and United States governments and the effect upon domestic farm workers.

"Sundering of the Grape Growers." *America*, 121(July 5, 1969), 4.
News item: success for UFWOC will depend on developments when the grape harvest begins in August [1969].

"Support For Delano Strikers." *Ave Maria*, 103(February 12, 1966), 16-17.

Sutor, Jack. "When Disaster Strikes: Florida Farmworkers Find Jobless Pay System Can React Quickly In An Emergency." *Manpower*, 3(October, 1971), 19-23.

Taylor, L.O. "The Effect of Agriculture Boycotts." *American Society of Farm Managers and Rural Appraisers Journal*, 34(April, 1970), 53-54.

Taylor, Paul S. "California Farm Labor: A Review." *Agricultural History*, 42(January, 1968), 49-53.
Brief history of "Agricultural Labor Pattern" in California from mid-nineteenth century to Delano. NLRA; LaFollette Committee; Commission on Migratory Labor (1951); Senate Subcommittee on Migratory Labor. Good bibliographic notes.

Taylor, Paul S. [*Continued*]
——— and Clark Kerr. "Uprisings on the Farms." *Survey Graphic,* 24(January, 1935), 19-22+.

——— and Tom Vasey. "Contemporary Background of California Farm Labor." *Rural Sociology,* 1(December, 1936), 401-419.
The growth of agribusiness.

——— and Tom Vasey. "Historical Background of California Farm Labor." *Rural Sociology,* 1(September, 1936), 281-295.

Taylor, Ronald B. "The Boycott and the NLRA." *Nation,* 208(May 12, 1969), 591-593.
Cesar Chavez, UFWOC, grape boycott, legislation, "greencarders," NLRA.

———. "Huelga! The Boycott That Worked." *Nation,* 211(September 7, 1970), 167-169.
Gives good background information on the grape strike and boycott.

———. "Nerve Gas in the Orchard." *Nation,* 210(June 22, 1970), 751-753.
Effects of pesticides on farm workers; efforts of UFWOC and California Rural Legal Assistance to protect farm workers.

———. "A Romance Rekindled." *Nation,* 216(March 19, 1973), 366-370.
Teamsters and growers.

———. "Why Chavez Spurns the Labor Act." *Nation,* 212(April 12, 1971), 454-456.
Coverage under NLRA, as amended by Taft-Hartley and Landrum-Griffin Acts, would prohibit UFWOC from using secondary boycott.

"Teamsters, Growers Renegotiate." *Monthly Labor Review,* 96(March, 1973), 73-74.
Contracts; California Supreme Court decision.

"Teamsters Sign With Growers." *Monthly Labor Review,* 96(June, 1973), 73-74.
Contracts with Coachella Valley grape growers.

Teatro Campesino." *New Yorker,* 43(August, 19, 1967), 23-25.
Farmworkers Theater.

"Temporary Halt on Boycott." *America,* 124(April 10, 1971), 362.
UFWOC and Teamsters reach jurisdictional understanding—lettuce boycott suspended for 30 days.

" 'There's a Union Train A Comin'." *Seafarers Log,* 30(January 19, 1968).
UFWOC strike and boycott against table grape growers.

Thornton, Richard V. "Farm Unionization Inevitable." *Canner/Packer,* 140(February, 1971), 28-29.

"Three Statements on the California Grape Strike." *Catholic Mind,* 68(October, 1970), 1-7.
Reprint of Fr. Daniel Lyons' editorial, "Chavez Reaps Bitter Harvest" (*Twin Circle,* July 12, 1970), which criticized both Chavez and the Bishops Ad Hoc Committee on the Farm Labor Dispute; and rebuttal statements issued by the Bishops Committee and by PADRES, an association of Mexican American priests.

"Throwing Tomatoes At the Colleges." *Farm Journal,* 96(August, 1972), 50.
Editorial. Criticizes Hightower's *Hard Tomatoes, Hard Times* (Washington: Agribusiness Accountability Project, 1972).

"Tio Taco Is Dead." *Newsweek,* 75(June 29, 1970), 22-28+.
Growing activism of Mexican Americans; Cesar Chavez, UFWOC, grape strike and boycott; Reies Lopez Tijerina, Rodolfo (Corky) Gonzales, Jose Guiterrez, and La Raza Unida.

Tobin, Richard L. "One Million Migrants." *Saturday Review,* 51(August 17, 1968), 12-15+.
Delano grape strike, UFWOC, Cesar Chavez, P.L. 78, AWOC, living and working conditions of migrant workers.

"Tortilla Fiat." *Time,* 98(July 26, 1971), 42.
Fr. Victor Salandini.

"Tossed Salad." *Newsweek,* 57(February 20, 1961), 26.
AFL-CIO strike in Imperial Valley lettuce fields.

Toth, Barbara. "Labor in a Year of Expansion." *Monthly Labor Review,* 92(January, 1969), 11-19.
Section of article is on UFWOC.

Tracey, Phil. "Cesar Chavez's New Revolution." *National Catholic Reporter,* 6(February 11, 1970), 3.
Review of Matthiessen, *Sal Si Puedes* (New York: Random House, 1970).

Triggs, Matt. ". . . Eat More Grapes." *Canner/Packer,* 138(February, 1969), 25-26.
Excerpts from speech to American Farm Bureau Federation by its Assistant Legislative Director.

"Trouble In the Melon Patch." *Newsweek,* 69(June 19, 1967), 38-39.
Texas; UFWOC organizing and strike; Texas Rangers.

"The Truth About Chavez: Why He's Hitting Pesticides So Hard." *Farm Chemicals,* 132(November, 1969), 32+.

Turner, William. "No Dice For Braceros" in "Bracero Politics: A Special Report." *Ramparts,* 4(September, 1965), 14-32. Reprinted in *Ramparts,* 7(January 25-February 7, 1969), 37-40.

"UFWOC Wins First Pacts With Table Grape Growers." *Advance*, 56(May 1, 1970), 2.

"Undanknuffade Arbetargrupp." *KommunalArbetaren*, November 3, 1968, 8-9.

"Unionization of Grape Vineyards Nears Completion." *Advance*, 56(August, 1970), 2. In Spanish, p. 10.

"Unionizing the Farm." *Business Week*, April 22, 1967, pp. 164-165.
DiGiorgio/UFWOC contract signing.

Upton, Don. "AWOC Boss Cites Grower Misconceptions," *California Farmer*, 224(March 5, 1966), 18+.
Interview with C. Al Green, Director of AWOC.

"The Uses of History." Citizens For Farm Labor, *Farm Labor*, 4(April, 1966), 5-6.
Editorial. By using samples from the LaFollette Committee hearings regarding agricultural strikes, 1933-1939, the editor propose that California Governors *can* take action to intervene in a strike.

Valdez, Luis Miguel. "El Teatro Campesino." *Ramparts*, 5(July, 1966), 55-56.
Farmworkers Theater.

———. "The Tale of the Raza" in "Huelga! Tales of the Revolution." *Ramparts*. 5(July, 1966), 40-43.

"Valley Workers Striking." *New Republic*, 118(June 21, 1948), 6.
Asparagus strike; Food, Tobacco and Agricultural Workers (CIO); Farm Labor Union (AFL); strike against DiGiorgio-Associated Farmer group.

Van Arsdall, Roy N. "Pay Perquisities, and the Wage Contract." *Farm Labor Developments*, August-September, 1967, 26-32.
"Growth will take place on the efficient farms that continue to specialize, use more and larger machinery, engineer the farmland efficiently, and manage labor effectively."

Van Buskirk, R.G. "A Positive Perspective on Pesticides." *Canner/Packer*, 140(February, 1971), 30-32.

Velie, Lester. "Poverty At the Border." *Readers Digest*, 97(August, 1970), 92-97.
Use of greencarders from Mexico; UFWOC; California Rural Legal Assistance; U.S. Immigration Service and immigration laws.

VeraCruz, Philip. "The Farm Workers and the Church." *Catholic Worker*, 36(September, 1970), 1, 7-8.

———. "A Farm Worker's Viewpoint." *Catholic Worker*, 36(May, 1970), 7+.
AWOC, Delano strike.

"Victory At Delano." *America,* 114(April 23, 1966), 579-580.
Schenley recognizes NFWA as sole bargaining agent.

"Victory For Cesar Chavez." *Newsweek,* 76(August 10, 1970), 56+.
Signing of contract with 26 major grape growers.

"Victory In the California Grape Workers Dispute." *Labour Gazette,* 70(June, 1970), 397.

"Victory In the Vineyards." *Time,* 87(April 15, 1966), 59-60.
NFWA recognized as bargaining agent at Schenley; support from churchmen.

Villarreal, Jose Antonio. "Mexican-Americans and the Leadership Crisis." *Los Angeles Times WEST Magazine,* September 25, 1966, pp. 44-50.
Cesar Chavez, Bert Corona. Conflict between youth and experience; Mexican community is fragmented.

"Vineyards of Strife." *Senior Scholastic,* 88(March 18, 1966), 18.

"Violence in the Oasis." *Time,* 77(Feburary 17, 1961), 18.
AWOC strike in lettuce fields of California's Imperial Valley.

"'Viva la Huelga!'" *Newsweek,* 67(April 18, 1966), 42-43.
Pilgrimage from Delano to Sacramento: Schenley, DiGiorgio.

Vizzard, James L. "The Extraordinary Cesar Chavez." *Progressive,* 30(July, 1966), 16-20.

———. "Families In the Fields." *Catholic Digest,* 31(February, 1967), 17-20.

———. "Grape Strike." *Commonweal,* 84(May 27, 1966), 295-296.

———. "The Long March of the Migrants." *Jubilee,* 15(May, 1967), 36-40.
Fifteen years of efforts to get legislation for farm workers.

———. "The Story of Cesar Chavez." *Catholic Mind,* 64(September, 1966), 33-42.

"Vote In a Field." *Economist,* 220(September 17, 1966), 1133.

Walsh, James F. "The Migrant Worker: A Changing Way of Life." *Catholic Charities Review,* 51(November, 1967), 4-9.

Walsh, Stewart. "Interview With Manuel Salas of Obreros Unidos." *Wisconsin Review.* 4(Fall, 1968), 2-9.

"War on the Poor?" *Newsweek,* 77(January 18, 1971), 18-19.
Governor Reagan vetoes OEO grant to California Rural Legal Assistance.

Watson, Mary Lou. "Boycott Seeks to Aid Grape Workers." *Christian Century.* 85(June 5, 1968), 769-770.

Weissbrodt, Sylvia. "Changes in State Labor Laws in 1971." *Monthly Labor Review,* 95(January, 1972), 29-39.

Section on agricultural workers describes new state laws, both proposed and enacted.

West, Irma. "Occupational Disease of Farm Workers." *Archives of Environmental Health,* 9(July, 1964), 92-98. Paper read at 23rd American Medical Assn. Congress on Occupational Health, Sept. 25-26; 1963.
"In California, the agricultural industry experiences the highest occupational disease rate." Pesticide poisoning, tetanus, heat stroke, food poisoning, dermatitis, and work injuries.

Westerfield, Rex T. "La Raza: Now It's the Brown Revolution." *American Opinion.* 12(September, 1969), 43-54.

———. "Sour Grapes: The Move to Control Our Food Supply." *American Opinion,* 11(December, 1968), 49-66.

"Western Food Processing Division Wants NLRB Farm Workers Law," *International Teamster,* 68(Feburary, 1971), 78.
Teamsters, in urging NLRB coverage for farm workers, are "determined to resist all encroachment on the jurisdictions [they] now have in food processing."

"Whatever Happened to . . . The Grape Strike and Boycott." *U.S. News,* 68(April 6, 1970), 58.
Growers consider the strike ineffective because they can get all the non-union labor they want, but consider the grape boycott partially successful.

"When U.S. Barred Foreign Workers From Farms . . . ." *U.S. News,* 58(May 31, 1965), 73-75.

"Where Braceros Once Worked." *Business Week,* January 16, 1965, pp. 32-33.
P.L. 78 expires: California growers complain about lack of laborers.

"Where Does the California Grape Boycott Stand?" *Migration Today,* 15(Autumn, 1970), 61-63.

White, Jack E., Jr. "Chavez Begins Lettuce Boycott." *Race Relations Reporter,* No. 18, October 16, 1970, n.p.
Attempts by UFWOC to organize Salinas Valley lettuce workers; lettuce boycott; Teamsters. Also gives background information on Chavez, UFWOC, and the grape boycott.

"Who is Cesar Chavez?" *Catholic Boy,* 38(September, 1969), 41-43.
Brief biographical sketch of Chavez and his efforts to organize farm workers.

"Who Pays For the Celery?" *Social Service Review,* 39(June, 1965), 234-235.

"Who'll Pick the Strawberries?" *Time,* 85(June 4, 1965), 19-20.
Braceros, minimum wage, immigration laws.

"Why Unions Are Boycotting Lettuce." *American Teacher,* 57(November, 1972), 9-10.
Background information and outline for teaching unit.

"Will Growers Get Mexican Labor?" *U.S. News*, 58(April 5, 1965), 93-94.
End of bracero program.

"Will Mr. Chavez Finally Prevail?" *America*, 118(March 23, 1968), 366.

Williams, Doran. "Starr County Strike." *Social Progress*. 59(May-June, 1969), 25-29.

Williams, Harrison A., Jr. "The Migratory Farm Worker." *Labor Today*, 6(June-July, 1967), 5-8.
Minimum wage, housing, education, farm labor contractors, child labor, collective bargaining.

Wilson, Mildred G. "The Agricultural Minimum Wage in 1969." *Farm Labor Developments*, June-July, 1970, pp. 3-10.
General summary of agricultural wages and analysis of 17 states containing low-wage areas.

———. "Impact of the Federal Minimum Wage on Employment and Wages of Seasonal Farmworkers, 1967-1968." *Farm Labor Developments*, June, 1969, pp. 8-13.

Wilson, Thomas J. "Agriculture Committee Sees True Delano Story." *California Grange News*, October 15, 1969.

"The Wine of Victory." *Progressive*, 30(May, 1966), 5.

"Wirtz Helps Growers—A Little." *Business Week*, April 17, 1965, pp. 45-46+.
Permits entry of small numbers of foreign workers to help California and Florida growers.

Woell, Mel. "The Farm Worker—Man in the Middle." *American Farmer*, February, 1972. pp. 20-21.
Describes contents of an anti-UFWOC film, "The Road to Delano," made by the American Farm Bureau Federation.

Wolf, Jerome. "The Church and Delano." *Commonweal*, 84(April 29, 1966), 168-169.

Wolfe, Burton H. "Father Vizzard: Enemy of Exploiters." *Sign*, 45(May, 1966), 16-18.
Fr. Vizzard's activities on behalf of farm workers and rural poor.

———. "What the Farm Labor Battle Is All About." *Californian*, 2(November, 1961), 10-18.

Wollenberg, Charles, "Huelga, 1928 Style: The Imperial Valley Cantaloupe Workers' Strike." *Pacific Historical Review*, 38(February, 1969), 45-58.
Makes some comparisons between the 1928 strike and the present farm workers' strikes in California.

Womack, John Jr. "The Chicanos." *New York Review of Books*, 19(August 31, 1972), 12-18.
A brief history of Mexican Americans, followed by a bibliographic essay, review, and critique of 15 books dealing with Mexican American history.

Wooten, Paul. "Seasonal Labor, and Plenty of It." *Farm Quarterly*, 21(Fall, 1966), 42-45+.
Use of Puerto Ricans in New Jersey.

"The World of Domingo Arredondo." *UAW Solidarity*, 10(April, 1967), 11-12.
Farm workers' strike in Texas.

"Wrath of Grapes." *Farm Journal*, 93(February, 1969), 33.

"The Wrath of Grapes." *Time*, 93(May 16, 1969), 24.
Grape boycott, NLRB, Taft-Hartley, Cesar Chavez, UFWOC.

Yamamoto, Hisaye. "Food Caravan to Delano." *Catholic Worker*, 37(January, 1971), 5+.

———. "Story of a Grower." *Catholic Worker*, 36(May, 1970), 6+.
Strike at Seabrook Farms in Cumberland County, New Jersey, 1934: various unions and organizations involved; comparison with conditions in 1970.

Yinger, Winthrop B. "Viva La Causa." *Christian Century*, 86(August 27, 1969), 1115-1116.
Refutes many of the arguments of large growers regarding UFWOC and farm workers.

Zimmerman, M. "Mechanizing the Grape Harvest." *Agricultura De Las Americas*. 18(June, 1969), 10-13.
In Spanish.

Zon, Henry. "Huelga!" *IUD Agenda*, 2(January, 1966), 22-26.

Beverly Fodell received her B.A. degree (1963) from Wayne State University. She is an archivist in the Archives of Labor History and Urban Affairs, Wayne State University.

The manuscript was edited by Jean Spang. The book is set in Compugraphic Times Roman. The paper is Nashoba Antique and the book is bound in Tuscan Cover. Manufactured in the United States of America.